CYBERSECURITY ECONOMICS
FOR
EMERGING MARKETS

CYBERSECURITY ECONOMICS
FOR
EMERGING MARKETS

Estefania Vergara Cobos

WORLD BANK GROUP

Contents

MAPS

TABLES

Foreword

With approximately 5.45 billion people—about 67 percent of the global population—connected to the internet, alongside roughly 18 billion Internet of Things devices, economies, societies, businesses, and individuals have become highly dependent on the smooth operation of online systems. Although digitalization brings enormous economic and social benefits, our increasing reliance on digital technologies also introduces major risks. This is also the case in developing countries where the pace of digitalization often outstrips the necessary investments and attention required to build cyber resilience, leading to potentially debilitating consequences.

Through an innovative approach using advanced artificial intelligence tools to analyze millions of online news articles in 98 different languages, the digital research team has created a unique database of cyber incidents from the past decade, addressing a challenge to research in this field—the lack of comprehensive and publicly available data. The insights revealed an alarming reality: publicly disclosed cyber incidents are surging globally, with a 21 percent annual growth rate. This acceleration is most pronounced in Latin America and the Caribbean and across upper-middle-income countries. Moreover, this may only be the tip of the iceberg, as over 40 percent of cyber incidents are likely to remain unreported.

The economic impact of these trends in developing countries is significant. In 2022, Costa Rica experienced a massive ransomware attack that crippled over 20 government agencies, including the Ministry of Finance and Social Security. Lasting nearly two months, this incident prompted the first-ever national emergency declaration due to a cyber incident, shutting down key systems and costing the economy an estimated 2.4 percent of its annual gross domestic product (GDP). Without the financial and human resources to secure their digital environments, and lacking affordable, context-specific cybersecurity services, other developing nations risk encountering similar costly incidents in the future.

Cyber incidents are not just draining economies but also endangering human safety. Over half of developing countries experience at least one publicly disclosed cyber incident affecting critical infrastructure each year. These incidents have resulted in millions facing power outages, disruptions in medical services, fuel shortages, port shutdowns, and more. Data on publicly disclosed cyber incidents indicate that the most impacted sectors globally are finance, health care, information and communications, and public services.

Mitigating cyber risk is essential for driving inclusive, sustainable development and economic growth. This study demonstrates that a developing country that reduces its number of major disclosed cyber incidents from the top to the bottom quartile of the distribution—reducing that number from approximately 50 to 7 during the study period—could boost GDP per capita by 1.5 percent. Equally important, a more secure cyberspace fosters trust in the digital economy and protects the most vulnerable, including those at the lower end of the income distribution and small and medium enterprises.

While we cannot eliminate cyber risk, we can try to manage and mitigate it. To do this, we must collaborate to understand and assess the threat landscape and identify efficient solutions tailored to the capacities of developed and developing nations alike. A crucial component of this effort is the routine and standardized collection of data on cyber incidents. This will be essential for informing future research and interventions, including understanding the scale of the problem, enabling the deployment of limited financial and human resources to enhance cyber resilience in ways likely to have the greatest impact, and providing a means to better evaluate the effectiveness of these interventions.

Securing our digital future hinges on our commitment to efficient cybersecurity. It is not just an option. It is a vital imperative.

Christine Zhenwei Qiang
Global Director
Digital Transformation Global Department
World Bank

Stephane Straub
Chief Economist
Infrastructure Vice Presidency
World Bank

Acknowledgments

Cybersecurity Economics for Emerging Markets was written by Estefania Vergara Cobos, economist in the Chief Economist's Office for the Infrastructure Vice Presidency at the World Bank. The book integrates insights from collaborative research conducted with Hagai Mei Zahav, cybersecurity specialist, World Bank Digital Transformation Global Department; Selcen Cakin, assistant professor, Bogazici University; Hualong Diao, PhD candidate, Stony Brook University; and Baran Berkay Barakcin, data scientist.

Invaluable support and guidance were provided by Stephane Straub, chief economist in the Infrastructure Vice Presidency; and Christine Zhenwei Qiang, global director, and Casey Torgusson, program manager, in the Digital Transformation Global Department at the World Bank. This work was funded thanks to the generosity of donors to the World Bank Cybersecurity Multi-Donor Trust Fund, with the support of Bertram Boie, trust fund program manager. Special thanks go to infrastructure experts Vivien Foster and Mark Williams for their encouragement during the concept stage.

Acknowledgments are extended to the many reviewers who provided insightful feedback. External peer reviewers included Lawrence Gordon (professor, University of Maryland), Charles Harry (professor and director, Center for Governance of Technology and Systems, University of Maryland), and Daniel W. Woods (lecturer in cybersecurity, University of Edinburgh). Peer reviewers internal to the World Bank included Luis Alberto Andres, Andrea Barone, Anat Lewin, Yan Liu, Carlo Maria Rossotto, and Davide Strusani. The background work for this book also benefited from feedback from Giacomo Assenza, Ghislain de Salins, Neil Gandal, David Satola, Keongmin Yoon, and participants in the University of Maryland 51st Cybersecurity Forum, the 2023 Cyber Week conference at Tel Aviv University, the 2023 Global Conference on Cyber Capacity Building in Ghana, and the IV STIC Conference & RootedCON Congress Panama Chapter.

Special thanks to Mark McClure for expertly overseeing the publication process of this book and to Brenan Gabriel Andre for designing and producing the maps. Additional gratitude goes to the graduate students from Seoul National University—Daeun Hwang, Jaeeun Lee, and Jung Hyun Alexa Shin—for their valuable research assistance. Finally, acknowledgments are extended to any individuals or organizations that contributed to this book but were inadvertently omitted from these acknowledgments.

About the Author

Estefania Vergara Cobos is an economist in the Chief Economist's Office for the Infrastructure Vice Presidency at the World Bank, where she leads research on the economic and developmental impacts of digitalization in developing countries, including the realm of cybersecurity. Prior to joining the World Bank, she held academic positions, teaching economics at institutions such as Santa Clara University, Universidad de las Americas, and Stony Brook University. She holds a PhD in economics and a master's degree in game theory from Stony Brook University, along with advanced studies in computer science, which she integrates into her research on the economics of digital transformation.

Executive Summary

In an increasingly interconnected world driven by the rapid adoption of digital technologies and online systems, the critical role of cybersecurity cannot be overstated. As societies aim to harness the power of technology to boost economic growth, enhance public services, and improve quality of life, they face heightened risks associated with cyber threats. In this context, this book demonstrates that cybersecurity is essential for the socioeconomic progress of nations.

Despite increasing cybersecurity awareness, significant gaps persist. These gaps largely stem from a lack of thorough understanding of cyber incidents and their consequences. This issue poses significant obstacles in mobilizing resources for cybersecurity, particularly in developing countries with limited budgets and pressing social needs. In response to these challenges, this book offers pioneering analyses that (1) map key elements of the global cybersecurity threat landscape, (2) link these threats to the means by which economies are affected, (3) identify efficiency problems within cybersecurity markets, and (4) propose adaptive strategies, flexible policies, and decentralized governance efforts to foster innovation and sustainability amid ongoing change and uncertainty.

The Threat Landscape

Generating systemic knowledge about the cybersecurity landscape is challenging due to a global data shortage on cyber incidents, especially in developing countries. To address this gap, World Bank researchers used advanced artificial intelligence (AI) tools to analyze millions of online cybersecurity-related articles in 98 languages from the past decade, identifying over 30,000 publicly disclosed cyber incidents. Combined with data from the Center for International and Security Studies at Maryland, a comprehensive database spanning approximately 190 countries and 21 industries was produced. The findings reveal an alarming reality, unlikely to be solely explained by changes in reporting behavior.

As the digital age flourishes, the world has found itself caught in a web of cyber incidents that is increasing in both size and complexity. From 2014 to 2023, disclosed cyber incidents worldwide grew at an average annual rate of 21 percent, with upper-middle-income countries experiencing the highest surge, with a growth rate of 37 percent.[1] Meanwhile, high-income countries (HICs) and lower-middle-income countries experienced growth rates of 22 and 17 percent, respectively. The increasing trend of disclosed cyber incidents over the past decade has been fueled mainly by the COVID-19 pandemic and the Russian Federation–Ukraine war.

Digital technologies improve economic and social resilience against a wide range of threats, but societies also need to be protected from them. For example, the COVID-19 pandemic prompted a rapid shift to digital infrastructure to facilitate online health services, education, social protection, e-commerce, telecommuting, and productivity enhancements. While these technologies provided significant benefits during a critical period, they simultaneously introduced serious cybersecurity challenges. Such is the case that, from 2019 to 2020, disclosed cyber incidents worldwide increased by 62 percent, predominantly affecting the public administration, health care, and education sectors.

Almost two years after the start of the COVID-19 pandemic and against the backdrop of geopolitical tensions, the ground invasion of Ukraine erupted, casting a shadow over the digital realm. The postinvasion period saw an astonishing 80 percent surge in disclosed cyber incidents from 2021 to 2022, particularly affecting countries in Europe and Central Asia, such as Italy, Lithuania, and Poland, and critical sectors like utilities and information and communications. The Russia-Ukraine war illustrates how cyber incidents have become an integral part of modern conflicts, emphasizing the urgent need to design digital infrastructures that bolster resilience in times of conflict.

Developing countries account for approximately 30 percent of the world's publicly disclosed cyber incidents.[2] However, the surge and impact of cyber incidents could be more severe in these countries given their rapid digitalization, lower cybersecurity commitments, and political and economic instability. Notably, Latin America and the Caribbean (LAC) is the world's region with the fastest growth of disclosed cyber incidents, at an average annual growth rate of 25 percent from 2014 to 2023. This significant surge in LAC was associated with a 145 percent increase in Internet of Things devices, a 280 percent rise in e-commerce volume, and greater adoption of e-government tools post-COVID-19 in the region.

The global landscape of disclosed cyber incidents from the past decade reveals a complex and diverse array of incidents shaped by various interconnected factors (Harry and Gallagher 2018). Approximately 61 percent of these incidents worldwide were exploitive in nature, as were 63 percent of incidents in HICs and 49 percent in developing countries. The remaining incidents were disruptive,[3] characterized by a highly stochastic trend, which adds a layer of uncertainty.

Financial motives dominate the landscape, accounting for 74 percent of disclosed cyber incidents globally and 80 percent in HICs. In stark contrast, only 41 percent of disclosed incidents in developing countries were primarily financially driven. The remaining shares of disclosed cyber incidents (20 percent in HICs and 59 percent in developing countries) exhibited political motives, ranging from protests to political espionage. Across industries, these differences persist, with HICs exhibiting the largest share of disclosed incidents in health care, and developing countries displaying a concentration of disclosed incidents of about 30 percent in public administration. These findings align with the generally lower levels of political stability in developing countries. However, they also raise concerns about the lack of incident disclosure requirements for the private sector in these countries.

Worldwide, cyber risk varies significantly, with countries facing different levels of exposure to cyber threats and varying degrees of cybersecurity commitments. HICs, such as the United States and the United Kingdom, have the highest exposure to cyber threats. However, various middle-income countries could be facing the highest levels of relative cyber risk due to their above-median exposure paired with below-median protection levels. Cybersecurity commitments, which reflect the level of protection, are crucial for risk mitigation. In fact, between 2014 and 2023, the average annual count of disclosed cyber incidents more than tripled in countries with low initial levels of cybersecurity commitments and doubled in those with high commitment levels. However, low-income countries have made the greatest improvements in commitments recently.

The Economic Costs of Cyber Incidents

The escalating frequency and costs of cyber incidents worldwide are alarming, posing real risks to macroeconomic stability, especially for developing countries. And what we know is likely just the tip of the iceberg, as many cyber incidents remain undisclosed. The economic impact of cyber incidents is potentially more severe in developing countries, where estimates suggest that the average disclosed cyber incident has a larger impact than in HICs.

Reducing the frequency of major cyber incidents is necessary for achieving inclusive and sustainable development, as well as economic growth. Recent research suggests that a developing country that reduces its major disclosed cyber incidents from the top quartile of the distribution (around 50 disclosed cyber incidents) to the bottom quartile (around 7 disclosed cyber incidents) in a decade could see an increase in gross domestic product (GDP) per capita of approximately 1.5 percent. Likewise, stronger national cybersecurity commitments could have positive economic effects, with estimates showing that more digitalized industries perform better in countries with higher levels of cybersecurity commitments than in those with lower levels, all else equal.

The onset of the COVID-19 pandemic amplified not only the frequency but also the impact of cyber incidents, with substantial increases in the average unit costs. For example, from 2022 to 2023, the average cost of a ransomware attack surged by 13 percent, and in the following year the average cost of data breaches climbed by almost 10 percent. These increments disproportionately affect small and medium enterprises (SMEs) worldwide, with large businesses (with more than 10,000 employees) seeing decreases in the unit costs of data breaches (IBM 2023, 2024).

The systemic nature of cyber risk means that even a single incident can trigger widespread disruptions. Such was the case of the 2017 NotPetya cyberattack, which resulted in more than US$7.3 billion in consumer losses, a figure that is four times larger than the initial drop in profits reported by the firms that were directly hit (Crosignani, Macchiavelli, and Silva 2023). The systemic nature of cyber risk could lead to dangerous scenarios like "cyber runs"—rapid, large-scale compromises of the financial and operational stability of the banking sector, which so far have been prevented thanks to proactive measures adopted by banks and regulators.

As cyber threats grow, the consequences extend beyond mere financial losses to broader national security concerns and the protection of people's rights, including privacy and access to essential services. This issue underscores the urgent need for efficient cybersecurity measures to safeguard economic stability and societal well-being.

The Cybersecurity Market

The cybersecurity market is experiencing remarkable growth and transformation, driven by factors such as the widespread adoption of cloud technologies and the emergence of new security challenges, such as those associated with the advancements in large language models and other AI tools. These dynamics are reshaping how organizations approach and invest in securing their digital assets and sensitive information. In 2024, global spending on information security and risk management is expected to increase by 14 percent compared to 2023 (Gartner 2024), reaching nearly 0.2 percent of the world's GDP. The areas experiencing the highest growth rates include cloud security and data privacy. However, security services, such as consulting and outsourcing, continue to dominate cybersecurity spending, underscoring the critical role that expert support plays in cybersecurity.

Despite its growth, the industry faces significant hurdles, including a shortfall in research and development (R&D) investment, indispensable for facing the new and advanced threats, and a pervasive global shortage of skilled cybersecurity professionals, with more than 4 million unfilled cybersecurity positions in 2023 (ISC2 2023). The cybersecurity workforce shortage is particularly affecting nonmilitary government sectors, SMEs, and developing nations.

Moreover, varying accessibility to cybersecurity markets may be giving HICs and larger businesses comparative advantages as societies progress in the digital era. North America commands over 50 percent of the global market, with a demand that is 16 times larger than that of all the countries in LAC together. The skewed market demand is also evident at the governmental levels, with government per capita spending on cybersecurity in HICs like Canada and the United States exceeding US$30, compared to less than US$1 in highly targeted developing countries like India and Mexico. In the business world, large companies are leading in cybersecurity spending. Meanwhile, top cybersecurity vendors report decreasing sales to SMEs, a phenomenon primarily due to a lack of resources.

The previously mentioned challenges could be further aggravated by various sources of market inefficiency:

- *Noninternalized third-party cyber risk*. Organizations that experience a cyber incident are often exposed due to a third party. Yet, this does not lead to increased investment in extended risk management.

- *Unclear returns on investment*. Unlike other cost-saving investments, the financial benefits of cybersecurity are unclear and even impossible to quantify with the usual cost-benefit approach, obstructing efficient resource allocation.

- *Moral hazard*. The majority of compromised firms pass losses from cyber incidents on to consumers through price hikes, while shareholders suffer from declines in market value.

- *Misaligned incentives*. Undisclosed cyber incidents, coupled with low public awareness and a highly competitive technology market, result in misaligned incentives for producing resilient digital technologies.

- *Information asymmetries*. The general population lags in cybersecurity knowledge and awareness. Moreover, it is practically unfeasible to assess the level of cyber risk or the effectiveness of cybersecurity products before a cyberattack.

Market inefficiencies could be more pronounced in developing countries given the influence of governments in HICs on global market dynamics through their large procurements and operationalized regulations and standards. Governments could address these challenges, for example, by prioritizing awareness and training programs and coordinating an R&D plan tailored to the country's needs.

Conclusions and Policy Recommendations

Cybersecurity represents a collective responsibility that must be shared by all economic actors. This book delves into pivotal aspects of cybersecurity, including the threat landscape and its associated costs, market failures, and the critical roles of governments. By providing new evidence on the socioeconomic impact of cyber incidents, the book argues that a safe cyberspace is key for unlocking the full potential of digital technologies and paving the way for inclusive and sustainable development in the digital age.

Developing nations in particular face the dual task of fostering digitalization and safeguarding against cyber threats. Recommendations for these nations include implementing safe data collection practices to support evidence-based tailored policies; promoting the development of a national cybersecurity industry; drafting action plans that involve different sectors and stakeholders; prioritizing resilience in critical sectors; and supporting cybersecurity awareness and training programs. The policy suggestions stress the importance of prioritizing cybersecurity in highly technological, operational, and financially interconnected sectors, like finance and communications, as well as highly attractive sectors, such as health care and public administration. The recommendations also include promoting inclusive research efforts in the realms of cybersecurity and cybersecurity economics, and monitoring both the short- and long-term economic impacts of cyber incidents. Additionally, the advice emphasizes supporting a strategic and tailored R&D plan, affordable provisions for SMEs, regulatory frameworks for data protection, fostering international collaboration and public-private partnerships, as well as monitoring the development and adoption of emerging technologies such as cloud computing and advanced AI. Finally, the policy suggestions are directed toward promoting proactive engagements in cybersecurity to protect critical infrastructure and essential services.

Notes

1. In this book, a *cyber incident* is an event or the end result of any single unauthorized effort taken using an information system (for example, computer technology) or a network that resulted in an actual or potential nationally relevant adverse effect on any of the three layers that constitute cyberspace—information systems, networks, and the information residing therein (Harry and Gallagher 2018; NIST, n.d.).

2. Throughout this book, the term *developing countries* is used to refer to nations that are not classified as high-income countries (HICs).

3. The Center for International and Security Studies at Maryland defines two main types of cyber incidents, "disruptive" and "exploitive." A *disruptive incident* impedes the target organization's normal operations, and an *exploitive incident* illicitly accesses or exfiltrates sensitive information, such as personally identifiable information, classified information, or financial data.

References

Crosignani, M., M. Macchiavelli, and A. F. Silva. 2023. "Pirates without Borders: The Propagation of Cyberattacks through Firms' Supply Chains." *Journal of Financial Economics* 147 (2): 432–48.

Gartner. 2024. "Planning for GenAI Initiatives Is Helping to Drive IT Spending in 2024 and Beyond." Gartner, San Francisco, CA (accessed July 21, 2024), https://www.gartner.com/en/newsroom/press-releases/2024-04-16-gartner-forecast-worldwide-it-spending-to-grow-8-percent-in-2024#:~:text=Worldwide%20IT%20spending%20is%20expected,the%20end%20of%20the%20decade.

Harry, C., and N. Gallagher. 2018. "Classifying Cyber Events." *Journal of Information Warfare* 17 (3): 17–31.

IBM. 2023. "2023 Cost of a Data Breach." IBM, Armonk, NY.

IBM. 2024. "2024 Cost of a Data Breach." IBM, Armonk, NY.

ISC2 (International Information System Security Certification Consortium). 2023. "How the Economy, Skills Gap and Artificial Intelligence Are Challenging the Global Cybersecurity Workforce." ISC2, Alexandria, VA.

NIST (National Institute of Standards and Technology). n.d. "NIST Glossary." Definition of Cyberspace. NIST, Gaithersburg, MD. https://csrc.nist.gov/glossary/term/cyberspace.

Abbreviations

AI	artificial intelligence
CISSM	Center for International and Security Studies at Maryland
COVID-19	coronavirus disease 2019
CRP	Cybersecurity Readiness Profile
EAP	East Asia and Pacific
ECA	Europe and Central Asia
GCI	Global Cybersecurity Index
GDP	gross domestic product
GDPR	General Data Protection Regulation (European Union)
GNI	gross national income
GSMA	Global System for Mobile Communications Association
HIC	high-income country
ICT	information and communication technology
IT	information technology
ITU	International Telecommunication Union
LAC	Latin America and the Caribbean
LIC	low-income country
LMIC	lower-middle-income country
MDCE	Media-Disclosed Cyber Events
MENA	Middle East and North Africa
NA	North America
NIST	National Institute of Standards and Technology (United States)
OECD	Organisation for Economic Co-operation and Development
R&D	research and development
SA	South Asia
SMEs	small and medium enterprises
SSA	Sub-Saharan Africa
UMIC	upper-middle-income country

Introduction

In 2022, Costa Rica fell victim to a major systemic ransomware attack that compromised the information technology systems of about 26 government agencies, including the Ministry of Finance, the Costa Rican Social Security Fund, and the Virtual Tax Administration. This systemic attack lasted for almost two months, during which, for the first time in history, a government declared a state of national emergency due to a cyberattack, shutting down the computer systems used for collecting taxes, controlling customs, serving beneficiaries, and more, and costing the country's economy approximately 2.4 percent of its annual gross domestic product.[1] The Costa Rican attack happened just months after two of the most significant cyber incidents in US history took place. One was the May 2021 Colonial Pipeline ransomware attack, which caused a six-day stoppage of the largest fuel pipeline in the country, leading to gasoline panic buying, fuel shortages, and price increases in several southwestern states. The other was the SolarWinds attack, which compromised the computer systems of several US federal agencies, including the Department of Homeland Security and the National Security Agency, as well as Fortune 500 companies and critical infrastructure providers. The breach went unnoticed for several months. Meanwhile, on the other side of the world, a major cyber incident in Albania destroyed sensitive public data, shut down government websites, and paralyzed most of the government services that had previously been brought online, including tax payments and civil registries. *In 2024, it is evident that cyber incidents can lead to devastating consequences for the progress of nations, although the full spectrum of the costs incurred and the broader economic, societal, and humanitarian effects have yet to be understood.*

The digital era has created growth and development opportunities; however, the interconnectedness in which we live has also undermined security. Currently, more than 5.4 billion individuals and millions of groups and organizations regularly use the internet. From digital networks optimizing traffic lights to systems monitoring essential services such as power grids and water treatment plants, nearly all aspects of daily life rely on the smooth operation of online systems and digital technologies. However, cyber incidents persist and are expected to grow in sophistication and disruptiveness despite the efforts of governments and stakeholders to protect cyberspace. *The general response to cyber incidents has been to invest more in cybersecurity, but how to do so effectively and efficiently constitutes one of the greatest challenges of this era.*

This book aims to contribute to the efforts to optimize and derive value from cybersecurity investments through a risk-based approach, revealing the diverse threat landscape around the world, the link between cybersecurity and economic outcomes, and key considerations for private and public stakeholders, especially in emerging economies. The messages of this work confirm that cybersecurity is an economic matter of high relevance for the socioeconomic progress of nations.

Thinking about cybersecurity economics requires an understanding of the landscape of realized cyber incidents as the midpoint on the path from threats to harm, which is affected by endowed exposure factors and cybersecurity measures. This framework combines the determinants of cyber incidents (for example, exposure variables) and the resulting factors (for example, economic harm), with cybersecurity as the calibrating force between the two (figure I.1). Conceptualizing the economics of cybersecurity in this analytical framework, the book addresses key questions about the rationale of cybersecurity. For example, what constitutes a significant cyber incident? Why do cyber incidents exist and persist? How do cyber incidents differ worldwide? How do they affect the economy and the development of societies? What are the essential roles of economic actors, mainly governments?

Chapter 1 provides a first look at the threat landscape around the world based on publicly disclosed cyber incidents. The chapter describes trends and breaks down disclosed cyber incidents by geographic targets, income groups, types of incidents, motives, sectors, and more. The analysis of novel data on publicly disclosed cyber incidents highlights ongoing global cybersecurity challenges and potential differences between the threat landscapes of developing countries and high-income countries. By conducting a comprehensive literature review, chapter 1 also discusses the determinants of cyber incidents, highlighting the roles of socioeconomic factors, such as unemployment, political instability, and income, and showing that national cybersecurity is more than a technical concept, it is an economic matter. This discussion is followed by an analysis of relative cyber risks across nations that suggests that developing countries, especially some middle-income countries, may be facing the highest levels of relative cyber risk.

FIGURE I.1 **The cybersecurity economics framework**

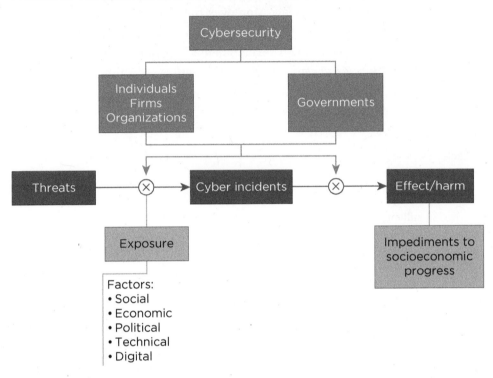

Source: Original figure for this book, based on Woods and Böhme 2021.

Chapter 2 discusses the economic effects of cyber incidents—including the direct costs incurred; the indirect losses, which, although harder to observe, are larger than the direct losses in the aggregate; and the overall socioeconomic impacts of cyber incidents and cybersecurity. In this sense, chapter 2 explores the "harms" side of the story, validating the belief that cyber incidents have the capacity to slow down the progress of nations in the digital era through multiple channels. These are (1) the economic channel, which includes financial losses, disruptions in the production chain, damages to reputation, and chaos in financial markets; (2) the digital development channel, which includes the erosion of trust in digital services; and (3) the social channel, which includes threats and loss of access to essential services and basic rights. This chapter also covers new research on the potential economic benefits of cybersecurity.

Chapter 3 discusses key market challenges for private and public stakeholders, particularly in developing countries. It describes the state of the cybersecurity market, examines multiple sources of market failure, and outlines essential government roles in protecting the infrastructure in cyberspace.

Each chapter includes actionable policy recommendations based on empirical analysis and a rich literature review. Moreover, the book concludes with key questions that can be addressed by future research to obtain a clearer understanding of the link between development and cybersecurity. In this way, the book aims to uncover key empirical and theoretical aspects of the economics of cybersecurity, to contribute toward prioritizing efficient cybersecurity, especially in developing countries.

Note

1. According to Datta and Acton (2022), the 2022 Costa Rican ransomware attack lasted 56 days, from April 17 to June 11, 2022. The local economy is estimated to have lost about US$30 million per day during the cyber incident, or US$1.6 billion in total.

References

Datta, P. M., and T. Acton. 2022. "Ransomware and Costa Rica's National Emergency: A Defense Framework and Teaching Case." *Journal of Information Technology Teaching Cases* 14 (1): 56–67.

Woods, D. W., and R. Böhme. 2021. "SoK: Quantifying Cyber Risk." In 2021 *IEEE Symposium on Security and Privacy*, 211–28. Piscataway, NJ: Institute of Electrical and Electronics Engineers.

CHAPTER 1

The Threat Landscape

Key Messages

Steady increase in disclosed cyber incidents

- Between 2014 and 2023, the number of disclosed cyber incidents around the world grew at an average annual rate of 21 percent and a median of 31 percent.

- This upward trend is expected to continue, particularly in developing countries due to high digitalization rates, lower political and economic stability, and insufficient cybersecurity measures.

Income-level variations

- Over the past decade, approximately 30 percent of the world's disclosed cyber incidents targeted developing countries.

- Upper-middle-income countries experienced the highest average annual growth rate of disclosed cyber incidents, at 37 percent.

- High-income countries (HICs) and lower-middle-income countries saw average annual growth rates of disclosed cyber incidents of 22 and 17 percent, respectively, during the same period.

- Developing countries mostly document politically motivated disclosed cyber incidents (59 percent), while HICs primarily report financially motivated disclosed cyber incidents (80 and 82 percent, with and without the Russian Federation, respectively).

Regional-level variations

- Latin America and the Caribbean had the highest growth rate of disclosed cyber incidents over the past decade (from 2014 to 2023), at 25 percent, followed by Europe and Central Asia, at 24 percent, and North America and the Middle East and North Africa, both at 11 percent.

Impact of global events

- Cyber incidents surged during significant events, notably the COVID-19 pandemic and the Russia-Ukraine war.

- From 2019 to 2020, the COVID-19 pandemic prompted a 62 percent global increase in disclosed cyber incidents, especially in HICs like the United Kingdom and the United States, driven by remote work and increased use of digital services.

- The COVID-19 pandemic highlighted vulnerabilities in the public, health care, and education sectors.

- The Russia-Ukraine war underscores the integration of cyber incidents into modern conflicts, highlighting the need for resilient digital infrastructure.

- Complex cyberattacks, especially on critical infrastructure, require significant preparation, making them less feasible during wartime due to the need for speed and control.

Sector-specific targets

- Publicly disclosed cyber incidents in developing countries are mostly in public administration (36 percent), followed by information and communications and finance.

- HICs present an even distribution of disclosed cyber incidents across sectors, with a slight concentration in health care (16 percent).

- The financial sector in HICs shows relative levels of resilience due to competitive cybersecurity markets and proactive market players.

- Worldwide, disclosed cyber incidents are proliferating across newly digitalized sectors like health care, education, manufacturing, and utilities.

Cybersecurity and political stability

- Countries with lower levels of corruption and higher political stability experience fewer disclosed cyber incidents.

- Moderate levels of corruption are correlated with 76 percent fewer disclosed cyber incidents versus high levels of corruption, and stable political climates see 81 percent fewer incidents than unstable political environments.

- Democratic elections worldwide are increasingly subjected to cyberattacks.

Developing country challenges (according to the International Telecommunication Union)

- By 2024, developing countries will have substantial gaps in cybersecurity commitments, particularly in capacity development, which includes fostering a competitive national cybersecurity industry and increasing public awareness.

- Between 2014 and 2023, the average annual count of disclosed cyber incidents increased by 3.1 times in countries with low initial levels of national cybersecurity commitments and by 2 times in countries with high initial levels of commitments.

- HICs went from scoring on average 36 points higher (out of 100 points) to 26 points higher on national cybersecurity commitments than their developing country counterparts, in 2020 and 2024, respectively.

- Latin America and the Caribbean has the lowest scores in national cybersecurity commitments among all regions, while low-income countries are presenting the largest improvements in recent years.

Introduction

Like land, water, or air, cyberspace is another environment that enables human activities, including those that support the functioning of modern societies. Created and manipulated by people, cyberspace is a giant network of physical and virtual information system infrastructures that facilitates the connection of approximately two-thirds of the world's population,[1] millions of groups and organizations, and more than 18 billion Internet of Things devices, a number expected to double by 2030 (Transforma Insights 2024) (figure 1.1). The increased level of interconnectedness and reliance on cyberspace is such that, directly or indirectly, nearly everyone depends on the accurate functioning of connected systems and networks, especially those used to monitor and manage essential services, including energy grids, transportation networks, water treatment plants, and telecommunications.

Despite the well-documented economic and welfare benefits stemming from the digital evolution of nations (Vergara Cobos and Malásquez 2023), cyberspace is a porous environment; therefore, a fundamental aspect of digitalization lies in the *expanding cyberattack surface*, which denotes the escalating vulnerability of digital systems and networks owing to the proliferation of potential entry points for malicious actors and cyber incidents (figure 1.2). Key factors that contribute to this phenomenon include the rapid digitalization of developing countries, which has led to more connected individuals; significant expansion of the number of connected devices; new security challenges posed by cloud computing and other emerging technologies that allow for data to be stored and accessed across multiple servers; fast software development; and gaps in users' cybersecurity awareness, among others.

FIGURE 1.1 Observed and projected numbers of Internet of Things connected devices worldwide, 2019–33

Number of Internet of Things connected devices (billions)

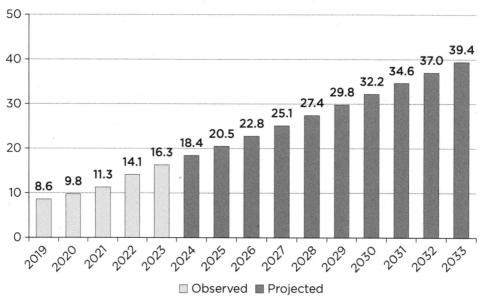

□ Observed ■ Projected

Source: Original figure for this book, based on data from Transforma Insights 2024.

FIGURE 1.2 Digital technologies improve economic and social resilience to a wide range of threats, but societies also need to be protected from them

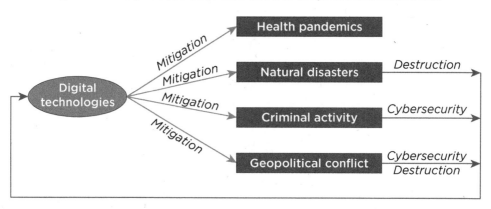

Source: Original figure for this book.

A core issue related to the expanding cyberattack surface is the technical vulnerability of the development of cyberspace itself. Cyberspace can be thought of as having layers that help in organizing and understanding its components.[2] One such layer is the logical or code layer, which encompasses the code, or the building blocks supporting the infrastructure of cyberspace (Ikwu 2019). Building a robust cyberspace infrastructure necessitates high-quality software characterized by a minimum number of errors or bugs. However, with approximately 6 million software developers writing code at every moment in time and almost none writing code completely from scratch (Evans Data Corporation 2023), the development of cyberspace is intrinsically vulnerable. Thus, secure software development is perhaps one of the biggest challenges of the digital era as it requires careful consideration of the many threats and mitigations involved. How can this situation be improved? Stakeholders could increase investment in automated vulnerability discovery tools, security education, improvement of secure development processes, and more. However, the key question in this and other cybersecurity challenges is to figure out what is the optimal or most effective intervention (Votipka et al. 2020).

The expanding cyberattack surface may soon become a significant concern for developing countries.[3] While these countries are experiencing rapid increases in connectivity rates, they have yet to encounter the full extent of cyber threats associated with achieving near-universal internet coverage and usage. For instance, between 2005 and 2023, the percentage of connected individuals increased by about 56 percentage points in developing countries, reaching approximately 63 percent of the population, compared to the increase of 35 percentage points in HICs, which have reached over 93 percent of connected individuals (figure 1.3).[4,5] Moreover, the expected cybersecurity challenges in developing countries could worsen if cybersecurity efforts remain slow-paced. This situation may require particularly urgent attention in Sub-Saharan Africa and Latin America and the Caribbean (LAC), where countries are currently lagging the most in capacity development cybersecurity commitments, with the main gaps observed in the development of a national cybersecurity industry, research and development, and public awareness and training (International Telecommunication Union, ITU).[6]

FIGURE 1.3 Evolution of the share of individuals using the internet in high-income and developing countries, 2005–23

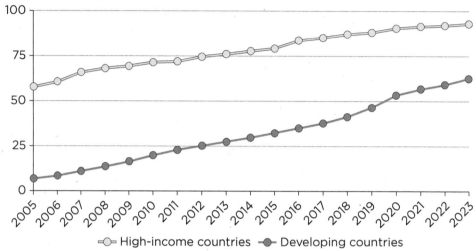

Individuals using the internet (%)

─○─ High-income countries ─●─ Developing countries

Source: Original figure for this book, based on data from the International Telecommunication Union.

Nevertheless, the vulnerability of systems and the continual expansion of the cyberattack surface do not guarantee that they will be targeted or that a cyber incident will occur. This chapter studies thousands of cyber incidents disclosed by media and other open-source outlets worldwide and shows that the prevalence and proliferation of cyber incidents go beyond technical reasons and include social, economic, digital, and political factors. (Annex 1A provides more information on the data sample.) Hence, although the technical aspect is crucial for cybersecurity, it is not the sole factor to consider, and it may not even be the primary aspect for understanding why systems face constant attacks and what should be done about it (Clinton 2023). This chapter also investigates the motives, targets, types, and frequency of disclosed cyber incidents, as well as countries' relative cyber risk. The analysis shows that cybersecurity is a multidimensional, heterogeneous, and dynamic challenge across nations that may face different optimization problems depending on their threat landscapes (map 1.1).

MAP 1.1 Post-COVID-19 change in the share of internet users and the Global Cybersecurity Index

a. Change in the share of internet users after the COVID-19 pandemic

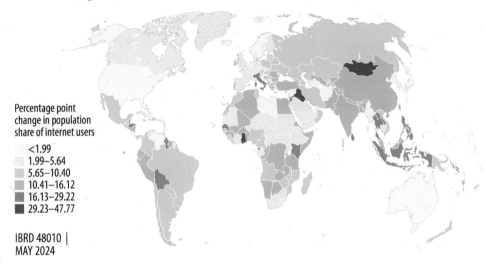

Percentage point change in population share of internet users

- <1.99
- 1.99–5.64
- 5.65–10.40
- 10.41–16.12
- 16.13–29.22
- 29.23–47.77

IBRD 48010 |
MAY 2024

b. Global Cybersecurity Index, 2024

GCI score (0–100)
- <14.23
- 14.24–36.60
- 36.61–58.02
- 58.03–78.75
- 78.76–91.25
- 91.26–100.00

IBRD 48045 |
SEPTEMBER 2024

Source: Original maps for this book, based on data from the International Telecommunication Union.
Note: Panel a shows the percentage point change in the population share of internet users from 2019 to the latest available year. GCI = Global Cybersecurity Index.

To mitigate and manage cyber risk, developing countries must plan for the expanding cyberattack surface by establishing tailored cybersecurity measures that target their unique landscapes.

Unraveling a Decade of Disclosed Cyber Incidents

This section describes the main trends in the proliferation of disclosed cyber incidents worldwide, the diversity of incident types and motives, and the sectoral landscape in developing countries and HICs.

Trends

One of the primary cybersecurity challenges that most countries face is the increasing frequency and sophistication of cyber incidents. Worldwide, the number of disclosed cyber incidents increased steadily at average and median annual growth rates of 21 and 31 percent, respectively, from 2014 to 2023.[7] Upper-middle-income countries (UMICs) have seen the highest growth rates of disclosed cyber incidents, with a 37 percent average annual growth rate, compared to the 22 and 17 percent growth rates in HICs and lower-middle-income countries (LMICs), respectively. The increasing trend of disclosed cyber incidents is projected to continue worldwide, although the proliferation is highly stochastic and dependent on social, economic, and political events.

Digital technologies brought a wide range of benefits during the COVID-19 pandemic (and other public health crises), but they also created serious cybersecurity challenges. Amid the COVID-19 pandemic, disclosed cyber incidents worldwide increased by 62 percent from 2019 to 2020, especially in HICs like the United Kingdom and the United States. The increase in the number of disclosed cyber incidents during the pandemic was primarily driven by the transition to remote work and augmented use of e-government services, telemedicine, and e-learning, which resulted in the information and communications, public administration, health care, and education sectors seeing the highest increases in disclosed cyber incidents during this period (figure 1.4).

The Russia-Ukraine war led to a further surge in disclosed cyber incidents of approximately 80 percent from 2021 to 2022, centered mostly in the involved countries and countries in Europe and Central Asia, like Italy, Lithuania, and Poland. For example, during this time, Poland experienced a record high of incidents, with a number of disclosed cyber incidents almost eight times higher than in 2020. These incidents included targets in more than 40 Polish public administration agencies and various transportation and warehousing operators. However, the surge of disclosed cyber incidents associated with the war began even before the start of the ground invasion in early 2022. As the war intensified, the aggressiveness and effectiveness of the disclosed cyber incidents decreased, demonstrating the quick and simple nature of modern cyber incidents in wartime. Sophisticated cyberattacks, especially those directed at critical infrastructure, require in-depth preparation and deployment. Therefore, they are less feasible during wartime, when attackers face a trade-off between speed, intensity, and control (The Economist 2022). In this sense, the Russia-Ukraine war illustrates how cyber incidents have become part and parcel of modern conflicts. Moreover, with information and communications being one of the primary targeted sectors, this situation shows how digital infrastructure needs to be designed to enhance cyber resilience in conflict situations.

FIGURE 1.4 Increased use of digital services during the COVID-19 pandemic

 Health
East Asia's "Smart City" technologies include digital tracing in the surveillance of at-risk individuals, AI medical chatbots, wristband-based smartphone tracking, and contact tracing.

 E-commerce
E-commerce rose from 12% in 2018 to 20% in 2021 as a share of global retail sales, particularly in Brazil, Japan, and Spain.

 Education
More than 110 governments partnered with the private sector, multilateral organizations, teachers, and local NGOs to bring digital solutions for remote learning **(EdTech).**

 Telecommuting
Close to 40% of the European labor force worked from home in April 2020. In the United Kingdom, the share rose from 5% in 2019 to 47% in 2020.

 Social protection
Countries that used digital identifications and databases for government welfare payments reached **39% more beneficiaries** than countries that did not.

 Productivity
In the United States, **27%** of Americans **e-signed** a document for the first time in 2020. In Peru, **agro-digitization** started showing great potential in the value chain.

Source: Original figure for this book, based on data from the International Telecommunication Union, the UK Office for National Statistics, and the World Bank.
Note: AI = artificial intelligence; NGOs = nongovernmental organizations.

A smaller peak in the trend of disclosed cyber incidents over the past decade is explained by political activism and cyber incidents in 2016 that exploited vulnerabilities in SWIFT, the global financial system's primary electronic payment messaging network (figure 1.5). Showing again that cyberspace might be the first environment to be involved during a conflict, a surge in the number of disclosed cyber incidents occurred three months before the 2016 Nagorno-Karabakh conflict between Armenia and Azerbaijan, in which the primary targets were the official websites of Armenian embassies and international organizations. In the same year, more than 20 Angolan government websites were targets of a systemic cyber incident motivated by political activism. This occurred while a series of cyber incidents involving the SWIFT banking network were reported. These incidents facilitated unauthorized SWIFT funds transfer requests between banks, subsequently resulting in the transfer of funds to accounts controlled by malicious actors.

The distribution and proliferation of disclosed cyber incidents across income and geographic regions is complex and influenced by a range of interconnected factors such as economic prosperity, political stability, cybersecurity capacity, and geopolitical tensions (map 1.2). For example, among low-income countries (LICs), Afghanistan, the Syrian Arab Republic, and Uganda face the highest

FIGURE 1.5 Global evolution of disclosed cyber incidents, quarterly, 2014–25

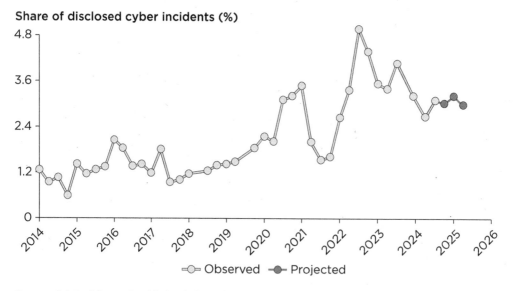

Share of disclosed cyber incidents (%)

Source: Original figure for this book, based on data on disclosed cyber incidents from the Center for International and Security Studies at Maryland and the World Bank.

MAP 1.2 **Distribution of disclosed cyber incidents, 2014–23**

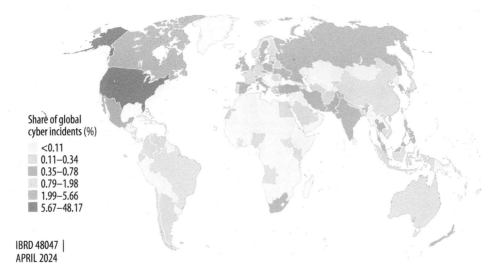

Share of global
cyber incidents (%)

      <0.11
      0.11–0.34
      0.35–0.78
      0.79–1.98
      1.99–5.66
      5.67–48.17

IBRD 48047 |
APRIL 2024

Source: Original map for this book, based on data from the Center for International and Security Studies at Maryland and the World Bank.

growth rates of disclosed cyber incidents, largely driven by political instability.[8] Conversely, among LMICs, Bangladesh, India, and Nigeria are the most targeted countries, with Bangladesh and India primarily presenting disclosed cyber incidents with financial motives, while Nigeria predominantly reports politically motivated incidents. Among UMICs, such as Brazil, China, Türkiye, and Ukraine, the motives of disclosed cyber incidents are more varied, mainly encompassing geopolitical, social, and financial motivations.[9]

Across developing regions, although East Asia and Pacific is the top target of disclosed cyber incidents, LAC shows an important postpandemic increase, as it moved from being the fourth most targeted developing region in 2014 to the second most targeted by 2022 (figure 1.6). This increase was driven mainly by the surge of disclosed cyber incidents in the information and communications and utilities sectors, as well as a large diversification to other sectors like transport, education, and health care. LAC is the world region with the lowest scores in cybersecurity commitments and the highest growth rate of disclosed cyber incidents over the past decade, at an annual average growth rate of 25 percent, followed by Europe and Central Asia, at 24 percent, and North America and the Middle East and North Africa, both at 11 percent.[10]

FIGURE 1.6 **Distribution of disclosed cyber incidents, by developing regions, 2014–23**

Share of disclosed cyber incidents in developing regions (%)

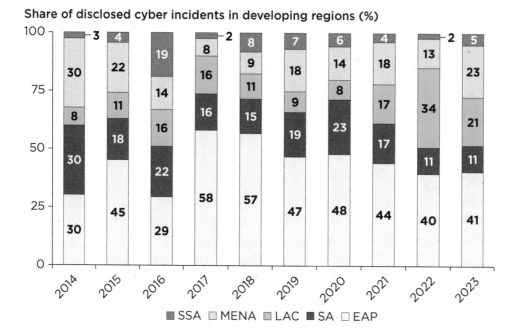

Source: Original figure for this book, based on data on disclosed cyber incidents from the Center for International and Security Studies at Maryland and the World Bank.
Note: EAP = East Asia and Pacific; LAC = Latin America and the Caribbean; MENA = Middle East and North Africa; SA = South Asia; SSA = Sub-Saharan Africa.

Among the main factors affecting the cybersecurity landscape in LAC, the share of internet users increased from 48 percent in 2014 to 76 percent in 2021;[11] the number of Internet of Things devices went from 407 million units in 2019 to 997 million units in 2023 (Pérez Colón, Navajas, and Terry 2019); e-commerce volume increased from US$176 billion in 2019 to US$509 billion in 2023 (PCMI 2023); and countries in the region adopted more e-government tools (OECD 2023). Notable disclosed cyber incidents in LAC include the following:

• *The Pemex ransomware attack in Mexico in 2019* severely disrupted operations and affected the payment systems of Pemex, the state-owned oil company. With a ransom of US$4.9 million, this cyber incident stood out as one of the costliest ransomware attacks in the history of the region at that time, far exceeding the global average ransom of US$42,000 seen across ransomware incidents worldwide in 2019. The substantial ransom underscores a concerning trend of escalating ransom values since 2019, likely propelled by the increasing sophistication of cyberattacks and the growing value of Bitcoin. Estimates suggest that the Pemex attack inflicted financial losses of between US$25 million and US$50 million on the state-owned company.[12]

- *The data breach in Ecuador in 2019* was one of the largest data breaches in the country's history. Through a compromised third-party system, the personal information of almost 18 million people, including minors, was exposed, potentially revealing full names, dates and places of birth, home and email addresses, national identification and taxpayer numbers, employment information, and financial information. The leak exposed individuals and companies to heightened risks of identity theft, financial fraud, corporate espionage, and various other security threats. However, the breach also pushed legislators to discuss a personal data protection bill in a matter of days after the cyber incident.[13]

- *Cyber incidents at banks in Chile in 2018 and 2020* compromised financial institutions, including BancoEstado, the only public bank in the country, and affected more than 10 million clients. The incidents led to disruptions of online banking services and the closure of more than 400 bank branches. Although the exact nature of the incidents was not disclosed, they underscored the cyber risks faced by financial institutions in the region.[14]

- *The ransomware attack on Telecom Argentina in 2020,* one of the largest incidents in the country's history, aimed to collect more than US$7 million in ransom. Around the time of the cyber incident, there was a significant, sustained drop in the company's performance in the stock market, potentially suggesting the presence of informed traders (figure 1.7).

Map 1.3 illustrates that population levels significantly influence the number of disclosed cyber incidents in a country. However, a closer examination of the number of disclosed cyber incidents per capita provides insights for other LAC nations grappling with cybersecurity challenges, such as Chile and Bolivia.

With the intensification of digitalization and the events of the past decade—mainly, the COVID-19 pandemic and the Russia-Ukraine war—serious cybersecurity challenges have emerged, with LMICs being particularly unprepared to face them. According to the ITU's 2024 Global Cybersecurity Index (GCI), which measures countries' cybersecurity commitments, LICs have a median score of about 45 out of 100 in terms of commitments, followed by LMICs with 63, UMICs with 66, and HICs with 94. In this sense, the levels of cybersecurity commitments are

FIGURE 1.7 **Evolution of the Nasdaq stock price of Telecom Argentina before and after the cyber incident in 2020, 2019–21**

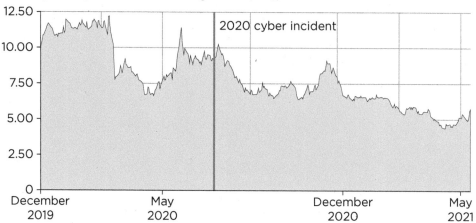

Nasdaq stock price of Telecom Argentina (US$)

Source: Original figure for this book, based on data from Nasdaq.
Note: The vertical line in the graph indicates the 2020 cyber incident in Telecom Argentina.

associated with the size of the economies. Although the gaps are closing, especially for LICs and LMICs, cybersecurity measures must be continuously updated to not further exacerbate the divide between countries with robust and weak cybersecurity infrastructures, especially if faced with other major economic, social, or geopolitical world events (figure 1.8).

In developing countries, the most advanced type of cybersecurity commitment is legal measures. Capacity building is the least developed type, with the largest gaps in research and development programs, government incentive mechanisms, and development of the national cybersecurity industry (figure 1.9).

Diversity of incident types and motives

Cyber incidents can be categorized as exploitive or disruptive, depending on whether the main target is to steal information or to interfere with some function of the target organization.[15] According to the sampled publicly disclosed cyber incidents, developing countries experience more disruptive and politically motivated incidents, while HICs experience mainly exploitive and financially motivated incidents. Between 2014 and 2023, the exploitive category accounted for 61 percent of disclosed cyber incidents worldwide, 63 percent of the incidents in HICs and only 49 percent of those in developing countries. As shown in figure 1.10, disclosed disruptive cyber incidents

MAP 1.3 **Distribution of disclosed cyber incidents in Latin America and the Caribbean, by regional share and per million people, 2014–23**

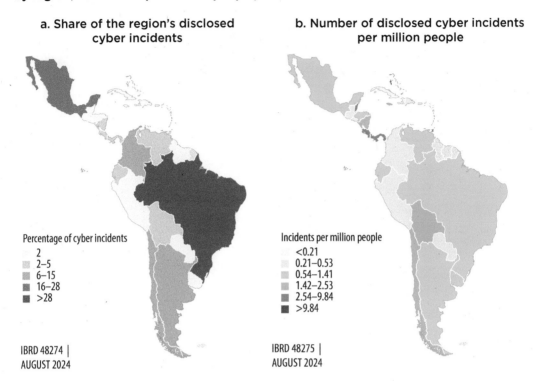

a. Share of the region's disclosed cyber incidents

Percentage of cyber incidents
- 2
- 2–5
- 6–15
- 16–28
- >28

IBRD 48274 |
AUGUST 2024

b. Number of disclosed cyber incidents per million people

Incidents per million people
- <0.21
- 0.21–0.53
- 0.54–1.41
- 1.42–2.53
- 2.54–9.84
- >9.84

IBRD 48275 |
AUGUST 2024

Source: Original maps for this book, based on data on disclosed cyber incidents from the Center for International and Security Studies at Maryland and the World Bank.
Note: The distribution of cyber incidents per million inhabitants in Latin America and the Caribbean includes countries with population greater than 200,000; thus, it excludes Guyana and Suriname.

typically exhibit more stochastic patterns that are linked to political and economic shocks. The relatively higher level of uncertainty holds even when removing cyber incidents linked to the Russia-Ukraine war. Interestingly, the COVID-19 pandemic may have affected the growth rate of exploitive incidents but not disruptive incidents.

Globally, 74 percent of disclosed cyber incidents are primarily financially motivated rather than driven by social or political factors like espionage, protest, or sabotage. The same is true for HICs, with 80 percent of disclosed cyber incidents having a financial motive. However, in developing countries, most publicly disclosed cyber incidents are linked to political reasons, like protests and political espionage, with financial motives representing only 41 percent of all disclosed cyber incidents (figure 1.11). This could be related to less rigorous disclosure rules of cyber incidents in developing countries.

FIGURE 1.8 Economies' cybersecurity commitments versus GNI, 2024

log GNI per capita, Atlas method (current US$)

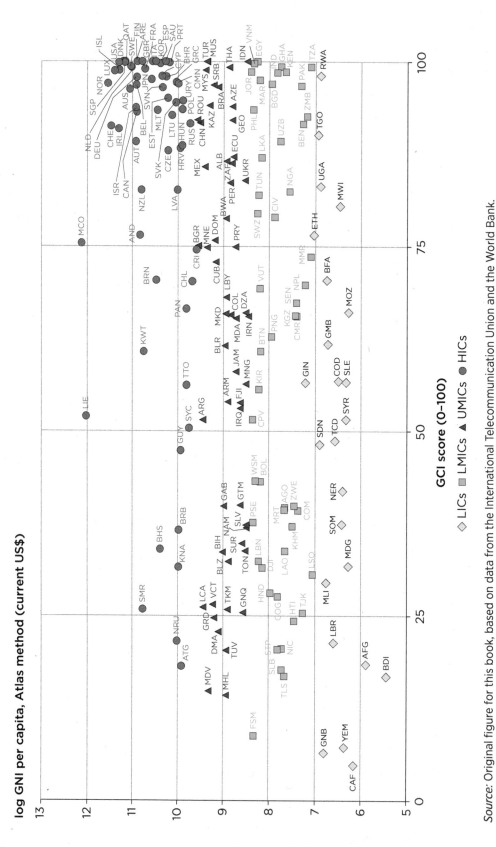

GCI score (0–100)

◇ LICs ▪ LMICs ▲ UMICs ● HICs

Source: Original figure for this book, based on data from the International Telecommunication Union and the World Bank.

Note: GCI = Global Cybersecurity Index; GNI = gross national income; HICs = high-income countries; LICs = low-income countries; LMICs = lower-middle-income countries; UMICs = upper-middle-income countries. For country abbreviations, see International Organization for Standardization (ISO), https://www.iso.org/obp/ui/#search.

FIGURE 1.9 Serious gaps in cybersecurity commitments across developing countries, 2024

a. Average by country income group (GCI component score, 0–20)

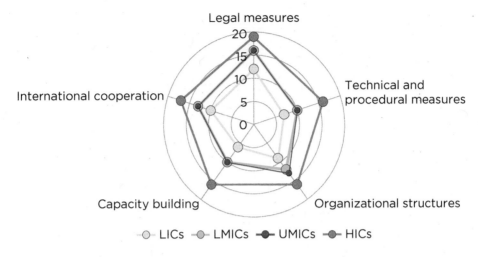

b. Average by world region (GCI component score, 0–20)

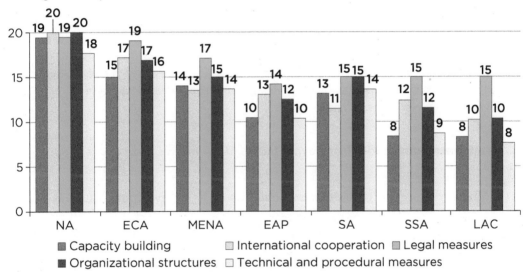

Source: Original figure for this book, based on data from the International Telecommunication Union's 2024 Global Cybersecurity Index (GCI).

Note: EAP = East Asia and Pacific; ECA = Europe and Central Asia; HICs = high-income countries; LAC = Latin America and the Caribbean; LICs = low-income countries; LMICs = lower-middle-income countries; MENA = Middle East and North Africa; NA = North America; SA = South Asia; SSA = Sub-Saharan Africa; UMICs = upper-middle-income countries.

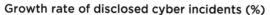

FIGURE 1.10 Quarterly growth rate of disclosed cyber incidents, by motive, 2014–23

Growth rate of disclosed cyber incidents (%)

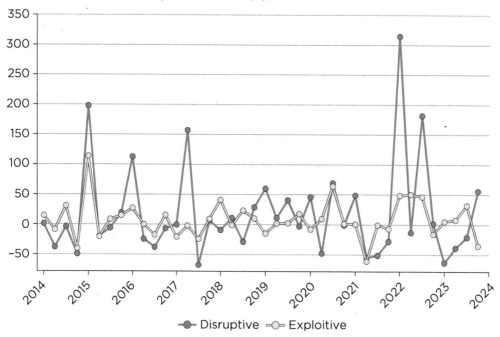

Source: Original figure for this book, based on data on disclosed cyber incidents from the Center for International and Security Studies at Maryland.
Note: A disruptive incident impedes the target organization's normal operations, and an exploitive incident illicitly accesses or exfiltrates sensitive information, such as personally identifiable information, classified information, or financial data.

FIGURE 1.11 Distribution of disclosed cyber incidents, by motive and income group, 2014–23

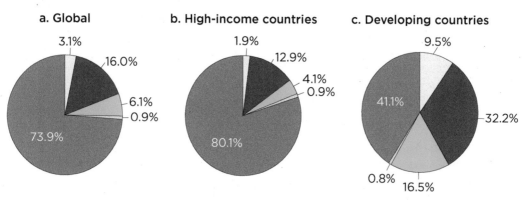

Source: Original figure for this book, based on data on disclosed cyber incidents from the Center for International and Security Studies at Maryland.

Cybersecurity Economics for Emerging Markets

Politically motivated disclosed cyber incidents can take various forms, and they are often aimed at influencing elections, undermining governments, or advancing geopolitical agendas. Research shows that the percentage of global elections subjected to cyberattacks increased from 10 percent in 2015 to 26 percent in 2022 (figure 1.12), mainly in North Atlantic Treaty Organization and Organisation for Economic Co-operation and Development countries, but also in developing countries like Bangladesh, Ecuador, Indonesia, Lebanon, and Malaysia, some of which faced the release of millions of voters' private information.[16] However, electoral cyber incidents may be related not only to data breaches, but also to the disruption of the functionality of countries' voting systems. This was the case in Ecuador in 2023, when the national electoral system was compromised, preventing most overseas voters from accessing the country's voting system before the polls closed.[17]

The landscape of disclosed cyber incidents across developing regions and countries is diverse, showcasing the different reporting rules established or the cybersecurity effects of countries' greatest challenges and digitalization levels. For example, in LAC, 73 percent of the República Bolivariana de Venezuela's disclosed cyber incidents are attributed to political reasons,

FIGURE 1.12 Percentage of national-level elections targeted by cyberattacks, 2015–22

Share of elections (%)

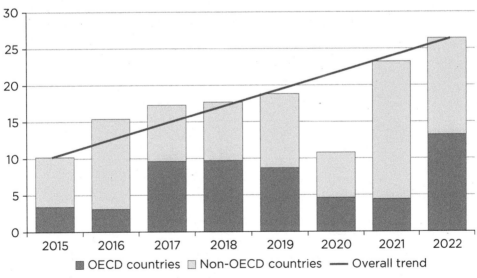

Source: Original figure for this book, based on Canada's Communications Security Establishment, 2023.
Note: OECD = Organisation for Economic Co-operation and Development.

while in Argentina, 89 percent of the incidents are linked to a financial motive (figure 1.13). Brazil receives over 10 percent of the world's ransomware attacks, has one of the highest levels of average economic losses per cyber incident in the world, and is largely targeted by financially motivated incidents (Kshetri and DeFranco 2020; Trend Micro 2023). Moreover, while the LAC region ranks lowest in cybersecurity commitments on average, some countries have made significant progress, notably Ecuador, with a GCI increase of over 60 points between 2020 and 2024 (see annex 1C).

FIGURE 1.13 Distribution of disclosed cyber incidents, by motive, in Latin America and the Caribbean, 2014–23

Share of disclosed cyber incidents (%)

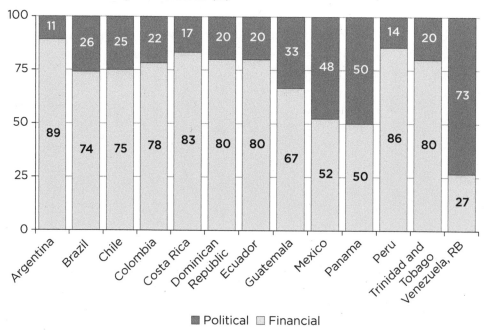

Source: Original figure for this book, based on data on disclosed cyber incidents from the Center for International and Security Studies at Maryland.

Sectoral landscape

On the one hand, consistent with the political nature of disclosed cyber incidents in developing countries, the data show a large concentration in public administration in these countries, followed by information and communications and finance.[18] On the other hand, disclosed cyber incidents in HICs are more evenly distributed across sectors, with health care as the top target.

The variation in targeted sectors is indicative of countries' economies, levels of digitalization, and cyber maturity, but also the attractiveness of the sectors to malicious actors. For example, in HICs, the health care sector is well digitalized and regulated (by the Health Insurance Portability and Accountability Act in the United States). However, this sector continues to struggle to provide cybersecurity measures that are appropriate for its high level of attractiveness, which is driven by the high confidentiality of the data that it handles and the criticality of its services. A notable example is the 2017 WannaCry ransomware cyber incident, which encrypted files on hundreds of thousands of computer systems worldwide, including those belonging to the National Health Service in the United Kingdom. As a result, several hospitals and health care facilities within the National Health Service experienced disruptions to their information technology systems and were unable to access patient records and critical medical systems, forcing some facilities to divert ambulances, cancel nonemergency surgeries, and postpone appointments (Ghafur et al. 2019). However, despite the efforts made to prevent similar cyber incidents (for example, enhanced cybersecurity measures such as network segmentation and endpoint protection in the systems of health care providers) (Al Qartah 2020), the health care and social assistance sector continues to lead in terms of the number of disclosed cyber incidents, representing a share of 16 percent of all incidents in HICs.

Even with its high levels of attractiveness and digitalization, the financial sector ranks sixth in number of disclosed cyber incidents in HICs, showcasing that in these countries cyber risk has been understood and managed as a threat to financial stability (Brando et al. 2022). Although it might seem that disclosure could be playing a role, banks and financial institutions in many HICs, like the United States, are subject to various federal and state laws and regulations that govern the disclosure of cyber incidents.[19] In developing countries, however, finance ranks third in the number of disclosed cyber incidents.

The following are among the good practices followed by the financial sector in the United States: (1) rapid investment in new and advanced security technologies (Mester 2019); (2) proactive risk management, conducting regular security audits and assessments to identify vulnerabilities in systems and networks[20]; (3) prioritization of employee training and awareness programs to educate staff about cybersecurity best practices[21]; (4) information sharing and collaboration with peers, governments, and cybersecurity organizations; (5) compliance with strong regulatory standards[22]; (6) development of incident response plans[23]; (7) investment in cyber insurance[24]; and (8) continuous implementation of monitoring solutions to detect anomalous activities before they escalate into cyber incidents.[25] Briefly, two key aspects of the implementation of cybersecurity in the US financial sector are

1. *A competitive market for cybersecurity products and services* tailored to the needs of banks and other financial institutions, supported by a diverse array of providers

2. *Strong regulatory bodies,* like the Federal Reserve System, which have supervisory and regulatory powers over the sector, enabling them to monitor and safeguard it proactively.

In developing countries, some of the most digitalized sectors are (1) the information and communications sector, driven by end user adoption of digital technologies; (2) the public administration, through e-government services; and (3) the financial sector, through mobile banking, digital payments, and others. Thus, it is no surprise that these sectors appear among the top targets of disclosed cyber incidents in developing countries, especially the public administration, which reports about 36 percent of all publicly disclosed cyber incidents in developing countries (figure 1.14). Assuming similar financial incentives across malicious actors worldwide, developing countries' financial and information and communications sectors might be showing alarming levels of relative exposure, compared to that of HICs, even with the differences in disclosing rules.

In terms of evolution and spread, over the past decade, disclosed cyber incidents have gone from being concentrated in a few sectors in 2014 (mainly in the public administration and information and communications sectors) to aiming at many sectors by 2023, especially the newly digitalized sectors (figure 1.15). Notable sectoral increases include health care, which represented shares of only 3 percent of the world's disclosed cyber incidents in 2014 and 22 percent in 2021; manufacturing, at 2 percent in 2014 and 7 percent in 2023; and education and finance, both at 6 percent in 2014 and at 10 and 13 percent, respectively, in 2023.

Worldwide, utilities, like energy and water, which constitute sectors of critical relevance for national and economic security, have seen important increments in disclosed cyber incidents, especially since the start of the Russia-Ukraine war. One of the first sophisticated cyber incidents targeting a utility company was the 2015 Ukraine power grid malware. It disrupted the operation of industrial control systems (for example, the supervisory control and data acquisition distribution management system) of three distribution companies, leaving approximately 225,000 customers without power for several hours (Case 2016).

FIGURE 1.14 Percentage of disclosed cyber incidents, by sector and income group, 2014–23

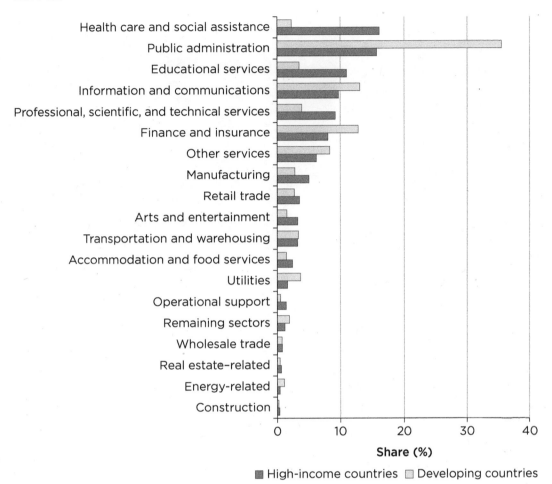

Source: Original figure for this book, based on data on disclosed cyber incidents from the Center for International and Security Studies at Maryland.

Although these can be seen as isolated events, cyber incidents that affect one provider of essential services (like electricity, water, or natural gas) could increase the cyber risk of other providers worldwide. This is because many of these providers use common networked commercial operating systems and applications, leaving them vulnerable to incidents like the 2017 WannaCry ransomware attack, which exploited vulnerabilities in a shared system. By 2024, cyberattacks on critical infrastructure like the energy grid are still used as political instruments.

FIGURE 1.15 Distribution of disclosed cyber incidents worldwide, by sector, 2014–23

Share of disclosed cyber incidents (%)

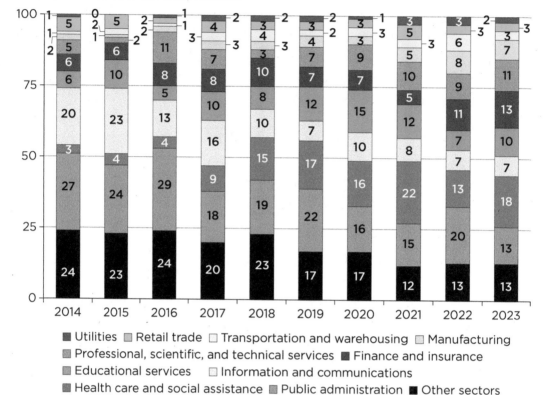

Source: Original figure for this book, based on data on disclosed cyber incidents from the Center for International and Security Studies at Maryland.

Although about 70 percent of the world's disclosed cyber incidents target HICs, some developing countries rank as the most attacked when disaggregating disclosed cyber incidents by sector (table 1.1). For example, India ranks among the top five countries with the most disclosed cyber incidents targeting utilities (second place), finance and insurance (fourth place), and public administration and educational services (fifth place). Ukraine ranks among the top five countries targeted by disclosed cyber incidents directed at public administration, information and communications, utilities, and transportation and warehousing. Other developing countries that rank among the top targets of industry-disaggregated disclosed cyber incidents are Colombia and Chile (mining), Brazil (real estate), and Mexico (other services). Controlling for population size, additional developing countries stand out as high targets, such as Armenia, Montenegro, and Moldova in the public administration sector.

TABLE 1.1 Top five countries, by number of disclosed cyber incidents in selected sectors, 2014–23

Sector	Top five targeted countries, by number of disclosed cyber incidents	Top five targeted countries, by number of disclosed cyber incidents per 1,000 people
Public administration	United States, Ukraine, Russian Federation, Italy, India	Armenia, Montenegro, Estonia, Moldova, Israel
Educational services	United States, United Kingdom, Canada, Australia, India	United States, United Kingdom, Israel, Ireland, Canada
Information and communications	United States, Russian Federation, United Kingdom, Ukraine, France	Malta, Lithuania, Israel, Latvia, Sweden
Other services	United States, United Kingdom, India, Mexico, China	United Kingdom, Bahrain, Israel, New Zealand, United States
Finance and insurance	United States, Russian Federation, United Kingdom, India, Ukraine	Malta, Bahamas, Latvia, Estonia, Lithuania
Retail trade	United States, United Kingdom, Canada, Italy, India	Singapore, United Kingdom, United States, Denmark, Canada
Transportation and warehousing	United States, Ukraine, Russian Federation, United Kingdom, Lithuania	Lithuania, Latvia, Estonia, Israel, Ukraine
Accommodation and food services	United States, United Kingdom, India, Italy, Australia	Singapore, United States, Ireland, United Kingdom, Australia
Utilities	United States, India, Ukraine, Italy, Russian Federation	Luxembourg, Lithuania, Latvia, Israel, Ukraine
Operational support	United States, France, Russian Federation, Australia, Italy	Australia, Switzerland, United States, Netherlands, France
Wholesale trade	United States, Ukraine, Russian Federation, Germany, Canada	Switzerland, Israel, Ukraine, United States, Canada
Real estate, rental and leasing	United States, Australia, France, Russian Federation, Brazil	Australia, United States, France, Canada, Italy
Mining, quarrying, and oil and gas extraction	United States, Canada, Ukraine, Chile, Colombia	Chile, Ukraine, Canada, Netherlands, República Bolivariana de Venezuela
Construction	United States, United Kingdom, Italy, Germany, Ukraine	United Kingdom, Ukraine, Italy, United States, Germany

Source: Original table for this book, based on data on disclosed cyber incidents from the Center for International and Security Studies at Maryland.
Note: The third column presents the top countries by disclosed cyber incidents per 1,000 inhabitants. This calculation was done considering countries that have had more than one disclosed cyber incident in a given sector, and a population greater than 200,000.

Diversity of Cyber Risk

It is evident that a system's vulnerability does not necessarily result in an attack. This implies that not all vulnerabilities are exploited and not all systems are targeted. Therefore, much of the literature on cybersecurity engineering tries to answer a key question: *what vulnerabilities lead to cyber incidents?* Meanwhile, the nascent literature on cybersecurity economics asks a follow-up question: *which cyber incidents matter?* (Clinton 2023).

Answering these questions requires considering all the possible determinants of cyber incidents. In this sense, research shows that cybersecurity is a multidimensional challenge that includes economic, political, social, digital, and technical aspects (figure 1.16). First, cyber incidents exist and persist because cybercrime is a lucrative business, which explains the exploitive nature of most disclosed cyber incidents around the world (Asal et al. 2016; Kigerl 2012; Kumar and Carley 2016; Mezzour, Carley, and Carley 2014). Second, cybersecurity breaches are a political weapon, and they are more likely to occur in environments with high levels of corruption and political instability (Kumar and Carley 2016). Third, cyberattacks are a response to socioeconomic struggles like poverty, unemployment, and income inequality, which incentivize cybercrime for illegal gains (Chen et al. 2023). In fact, research proves that unemployment has a causal effect on cybercrime rates, mainly in places with highly educated but underemployed computer experts (Hall and Ziemer 2023; Kigerl 2012; Kshetri 2010; Onuora et al. 2017). With higher levels of digitalization and more people gaining computer skills, this poses a particular threat to developing countries with high levels of unemployment. Fourth, as factors affecting the available attack surface, cyber incidents are also linked to digital and technical variables, such as the number of internet users and the available bandwidth (Kigerl 2012; Overvest and Straathof 2015). Thus, the determinants of cyber incidents, including cybercrime, constitute a web of social, economic, political, technological, and cybersecurity factors that are directly correlated with cyber incidents and indirectly related among themselves (Chen et al. 2023).

Indeed, a reduction in corruption and the establishment of a more efficient and stable political climate are associated with fewer disclosed cyber incidents. For instance, countries with moderate levels of corruption see approximately 76 percent fewer disclosed cyber incidents than those with high levels of corruption, and more politically stable countries experience around 81 percent fewer incidents than less politically stable countries, all other things being equal.[26]

FIGURE 1.16 **Determinants of cybercrime**

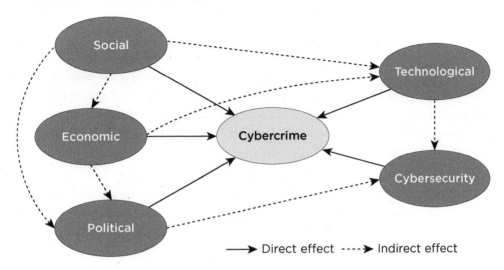

Source: Based on Chen et al. 2023, 3.

In this sense, cyber risk, or the probability of the occurrence of a harmful cyber incident caused by logical force, depends on determinants beyond technical measures. The concept of cyber risk has long been studied and discussed by scholars and stakeholders, who have identified several of its components, such as threats, vulnerabilities, assets, and potential harm. However, due to data and methodological limitations, a practical conceptualization of cyber risk is yet to be proposed. Although measurements of cyber risk are still under debate, it is widely agreed that effective cybersecurity solutions should strive to be conceptualized based on the relationship between three relevant components—threat, existing security, and expected harm—which together constitute cyber risk assessment, or an analysis of how a higher level of security translates into less expected harm given the threat level.

Cyber risk management also implies an amount of risk acceptance, which translates into a fourth basic variable for cybersecurity, *exposure*.[27] More exposure implies a larger porous environment, or a larger cyberattack surface, which could lead to higher levels of expected harm. Woods and Böhme (2021) suggest that effective cybersecurity measures are those founded on managing the relationship between threat and expected harm and moderated by security and exposure.

Practically, however, cybersecurity strategies and applications might not always be designed under this understanding of the threat, expected harm, and exposure.

For example, when stakeholders operationalize the computer emergency response team, there is usually little justification for how this will lead to reduced expected harm. The reason behind this is that measuring these variables is highly challenging in practice. First, a real measure of threat would imply knowledge of all the potentially harmful events (or forces) that can exploit a vulnerability and all the vulnerabilities in a system. Second, an accurate measure of expected harm would consider the direct and indirect costs of a cyber incident, including possible cascading effects. This would imply an assessment of the full spectrum of costs. Although researchers have made important advances in measuring the direct and indirect costs of cyber incidents (see chapter 2 in this book), the results come mostly from compromised actors, as there is almost no information on harm from uncompromised actors. However, although threat and expected harm are two components of efficient cybersecurity that are challenging to measure in practice, given the understanding of the determinants of cyber incidents, a proxy for *exposure* can be formed.

To this end, 23 pertinent standardized variables were selected from the fields of digitalization, economics, politics, and cybersecurity. Each variable was carefully chosen for its conceptual significance, support in the literature, expert insights, and data availability, and a pragmatic evaluation of relative exposure was constructed. The results show that HICs, like the United States, Russia, the Republic of Korea, and the United Kingdom, are among the countries with the highest levels of exposure to cyber incidents.[28]

This proxy for relative exposure, together with countries' cybersecurity commitments, based on the ITU's 2024 GCI, provides a plausible idea of the distribution of cyber risk across countries. According to this exercise, middle-income countries may face the highest relative cyber risks. Countries with a second order of risk are those with exposure and protection levels below the median (in the third quadrant in figure 1.17), including mostly LICs. Considering the rapid digitalization in developing countries (especially in LICs), the countries in the third quadrant could be pushed toward a riskier placement unless they continue to advance in their cybersecurity commitments. Finally, while most HICs appear in the first quadrant of highly exposed but highly protected countries, notable developing countries also appear in this quadrant, including Brazil and Mexico, the two most targeted countries in LAC. Due to the high levels of exposure in these countries, this group is likely to require more advanced and tailored cybersecurity measures than the ones included in the GCI.

FIGURE 1.17 Cyber risk clusters according to economies' relative cybersecurity exposure and protection levels

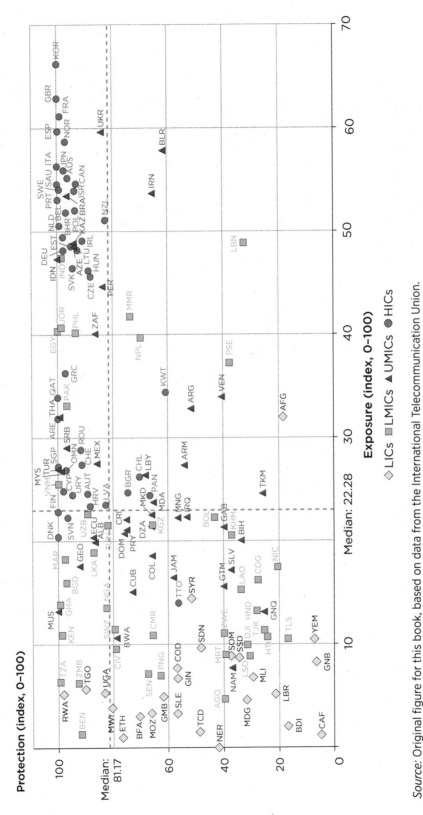

Source: Original figure for this book, based on data from the International Telecommunication Union.

Note: The figure excludes the outliers China, the Russian Federation, and the United States. Data for protection (y-axis) are for 2024; the years for the data on exposure (x-axis) vary. HICs = high-income countries; LICs = low-income countries; LMICs = lower-middle-income countries; UMICs = upper-middle-income countries. For country abbreviations, see International Organization for Standardization (ISO), https://www.iso.org/obp/ui/#search.

Data Availability: A Key Limitation to Achieving Tailored Solutions

So far, this chapter has shown that cybersecurity is more than a technical issue as cyber incidents are driven by a variety of country-specific socioeconomic, political, and digital determinants. The chapter has also shown that countries have different levels of exposure and protection. These insights imply that although countries can share a basic framework for cybersecurity commitments (for example, legal, technical, cooperation, and institutional measures), efficient cybersecurity solutions within a country should be tailored to the country's cybersecurity landscape (threats, expected harm, and exposure). Understanding the particularities of a country's cybersecurity landscape requires prioritization of data collection efforts that could help to motivate and inform research and policy making.

It is well known among cybersecurity researchers that a major challenge in the study of cybersecurity is the insufficient and fragmented data sets and statistics for indicators, such as cyberattacks, cyber incidents, and vulnerabilities, and the integrity of the available data.[29] Although in some countries victims are mandated to report major cyber incidents and specialized agencies are expected to record cyber incidents,[30] often these data present underreporting or underrecording of incidents or are simply not disclosed by the government (Howell and Burruss 2020). Although there is a relatively small market for data on cybersecurity collected in a variety of ways, like surveys and surveillance systems, there is usually limited coverage in developing countries, or the information is too technical to be translated into practical policy making (for example, data from assessments of vulnerabilities), or it has been flagged to have a commercial bias (Anderson et al. 2013).

The issues of data availability and data integrity in cybersecurity have prompted research in this field to focus on studying the cybersecurity landscape in the United States, through analysis of the Data Breach Chronology data set provided by the Privacy Rights Clearinghouse.[31] Published since 2005, the Privacy Rights Clearinghouse breach data are a longitudinal collection of reported cybersecurity breaches in the United States made publicly available by government entities (for example, government-maintained data sources like the US Department of Health and Human Services). Approximately 90 percent of the empirical research on cybersecurity uses the Privacy Rights Clearinghouse database and, thus, focuses on the United States alone (see chapter 2). This centralization of research could lead to a biased understanding of cybersecurity issues toward the experiences of HICs and a low uptake of evidence-based policy making.

Other major challenges in the current data collection efforts are the inconsistent definitions used to classify key cybersecurity indicators and the inconsistent measurement of consequences (Harry and Gallagher 2018). For example, the Center for Strategic and International Studies considers a major cyber incident as one that incurred losses equal to an arbitrary value of more than US$1 million; the Chinese government considers a major incident one that affects more than 10,000 users; and the European Union's General Data Protection Regulation is based on a broad definition of what constitutes a recordable cyber incident. These inconsistent definitions lead back to the questions of which cyber incidents matter and how to measure them.

Research around these questions, as well as efforts to collect consistent and reliable data, could help in finding quantitative evidence of the impact of the growing efforts to build cybersecurity capacity around the globe, a topic of high importance for stakeholders.[32] However, rethinking cybersecurity also requires a change in thinking about the returns to investments in cybersecurity. For example, the widely cited cost-benefit theoretical model for cybersecurity investments developed by Gordon and Loeb (2002) requires quantification of the probability of a breach and the value of the information being protected to find the optimal level of investment. However, given the data limitations, especially at national and sectoral levels, these two components can only be estimated under high-level assumptions. Therefore, it is recommended to explore alternative approaches to assessing returns on investments in cybersecurity, particularly considering the limitations of traditional cost-benefit models.

Policy Recommendations

Digital technologies enhance economic and social resilience against various threats, yet they also require safeguarding.[33] Hence, global stakeholders must acknowledge pivotal challenges in the digital era, including secure software creation and the increasing levels of digitalization in developing nations. Digitalization entails widening the cyberattack surface.[34] Consequently, nations must implement cybersecurity measures in parallel with the advancements in digitalization. Governments could consider the following actions:

1. *Conducting evidence-based policy making* informed by a comprehensive understanding of the country's main cybersecurity threats and expected harm. This requires governments to work on:

- Standardizing definitions of key cybersecurity indicators
- Creating incentives to achieve standardized reporting of cyber incidents
- Tackling the existing data gaps by diversifying data sources and including nontraditional data sets, at least until new data collection processes are implemented
- Advocating for data transparency
- Advocating for and supporting inclusive and tailored research.

2. *Closing the gaps in national cybersecurity commitments*, particularly those in capacity building, with a focus on strengthening the national cybersecurity industry.

3. *Switching the focus toward prevention and resilience* to minimize potential harm, especially during key periods such as times of high political activity.

4. *Developing long-term cybersecurity plans* that recognize the likely increase in cyber risk.

5. *Considering the best practices* observed in the financial sector in the United States, which include the following:

   - *A market approach* that fosters a competitive national cybersecurity market
   - *A regulatory approach* that establishes robust regulatory bodies that continuously monitor safety and stability.

6. *Prioritizing the most targeted sectors,* including public administration, information and communications, and finance and insurance, as well as health care.

7. *Designing resilient digital infrastructure,* especially in countries with high geopolitical risk.

8. *Considering alternatives in the design of efficient cybersecurity solutions* that acknowledge the uncertainties inherent in the quantification of returns on investment, including the following:

   - *Risk-based assessment* using both quantitative and qualitative factors to inform about the threat landscape and expected harm
   - *Scenario analysis* to evaluate the main cybersecurity threats and potential harm
   - *Dynamic risk management,* recognizing that threats are dynamic and evolving and require ongoing monitoring and adjustment of investment strategies
   - *Collaborative approaches* among private and public stakeholders to foster collective knowledge and information sharing.

Annex 1A: Databases of Disclosed Cyber Incidents

The study of cybersecurity faces a significant hurdle due to the scarcity and fragmentation of data sets and statistics on cyber incidents. To tackle this challenge, two databases on media-disclosed cyber incidents are used in the analyses carried out in this chapter: (1) the Cyber Events Database collected by the Center for International and Security Studies at Maryland (CISSM), at the University of Maryland (Harry and Gallagher 2018); and (2) the Media-Disclosed Cyber Events (MDCE) database built by the World Bank digital team using the Global Database of Events, Language, and Tone. Both data sets contain comprehensive details on each disclosed cyber incident, facilitating nuanced subsample analysis. Unlike other sources, such as data from private sector intelligence providers, media reports on cyber incidents are available across all countries, albeit in varying volumes.

The CISSM Cyber Events Database documents over 14,000 disclosed cyber incidents across 156 countries from 2014 to early 2024. Its construction involved three key stages. First, the identification of relevant cybersecurity online resources, such as cyber blogs and news sites recommended by practitioners, journalists, and academic researchers. Second, a script was executed to initiate online requests for gathering web data to populate the database. Third, manual validation of the events included in the database was conducted for quality assurance purposes. This manual verification process also involved gathering information on each incident's date, actor type, motive, threat actor country, targeted country, and industry.

The MDCE database was built by the World Bank team using a seven-step data mining process (figure 1A.1). This process led to the identification of approximately 30,000 disclosed cyber incidents in 179 countries from 2017 to 2022.

The CISSM database compiles information from major cybersecurity websites endorsed by experts, and selected telegram channels affiliated with hacktivist collectives. The database offers detailed insights into each disclosed cyber incident, including its associated industry, event type (disruptive, exploitive, or mixed), and motive. However, the database's reliance on English-language websites may skew the data toward high-income countries (HICs), with coverage of only 33 percent of the countries in Sub-Saharan Africa. To address these limitations, the MDCE database was created by scraping global media outlets written in 98 languages.

FIGURE 1A.1 Construction of the Media-Disclosed Cyber Events database

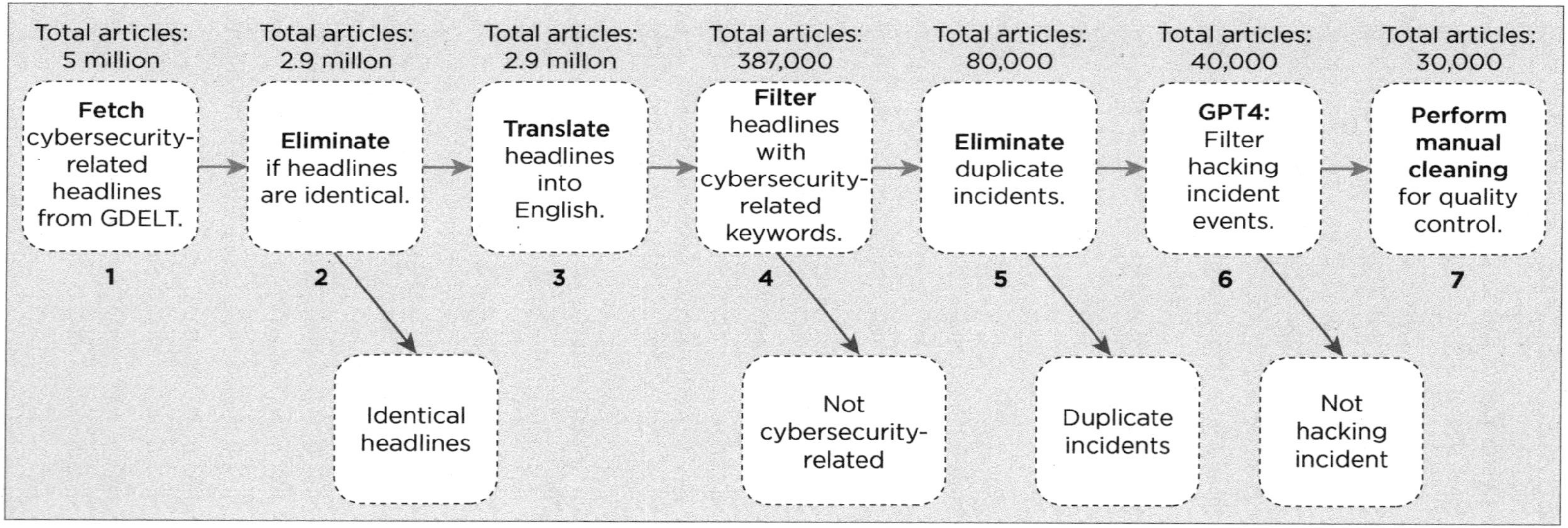

Total articles: 5 million — **Fetch** cybersecurity-related headlines from GDELT. (1)

Total articles: 2.9 million — **Eliminate** if headlines are identical. (2) → Identical headlines

Total articles: 2.9 million — **Translate** headlines into English. (3)

Total articles: 387,000 — **Filter** headlines with cybersecurity-related keywords. (4) → Not cybersecurity-related

Total articles: 80,000 — **Eliminate** duplicate incidents. (5) → Duplicate incidents

Total articles: 40,000 — **GPT4:** Filter hacking incident events. (6) → Not hacking incident

Total articles: 30,000 — **Perform manual cleaning** for quality control. (7)

Source: Vergara Cobos et al., forthcoming.

Note: GDELT = Global Database of Events, Language, and Tone; GPT4 = Generative Pre-trained Transformer 4.

Cybersecurity Economics for Emerging Markets

Although the MDCE database contains about two times more disclosed cyber incidents than the CISSM, their distributions across country income groups remain similar. Notably, the proportion of disclosed cyber incidents originating in HICs is lower in the MDCE database compared to the CISSM. Moreover, the prevalence of incidents in North America is notably higher in the CISSM than in the MDCE, suggesting that the latter may capture a broader spectrum of disclosed cyber incidents in developing countries, given its multilingual data collection approach. Another critical difference lies in the annual growth rate of disclosed cyber incidents, with the MDCE showing lower growth rates. Finally, sample analysis suggests that there is an overlap of cyber incidents of approximately 40 percent between the two databases. The messages reported in this chapter consider both databases (omitting duplicates as best as possible) or one of them, according to the coverage. The source(s) of each figure are stated as footnotes or notes.

Annex 1B: The Cybersecurity Readiness Profile

The cybersecurity exposure levels presented in this chapter were constructed by embedding 23 relevant digital, economic, political, and cybersecurity variables. Each variable was chosen based on its conceptual relevance, evidence in the literature, expert opinions, and data availability. Each variable was given a relative weight in the exposure calculation, based on the degree of correlation with global cyber incidents and expert consultation. Thus, the score for exposure in the Cybersecurity Readiness Profile (CRP) was calculated using a weighted average of the standardized cybersecurity, digital, economic, and political variables (figure 1B.1). The digital aspect incorporates variables that measure a country's digital capabilities, such as internet speed, network readiness, and investment in telecommunications. The economic profile measures a country's level of wealth and the sizes of the sectors that are more vulnerable to cyberattacks, including variables like gross domestic product (GDP) per capita. The political profile measures a country's political system, government structure, and conflict status. Political variables include corruption, political stability, and others. Finally, the cyber profile includes variables such as the total numbers of disclosed cyber incidents, major cybersecurity breaches, secured servers per capita, and rates of unlicensed software installations. The results present an exposure ranking that is consistent with the distribution of disclosed cyber incidents. For example, although it has a relatively low political exposure score, the United States ranks at the top of the country exposure list due to its high level of digitalization, financial attractiveness, strong economy, and high volume of cyber threats. The United States is followed by China, the Russian Federation, the Republic of Korea, and the United Kingdom.

The protection level of the CRP is derived from the International Telecommunication Union's 2024 Global Cybersecurity Index (GCI), which measures countries' commitment to cybersecurity and helps to identify gaps in their cybersecurity postures. A country's commitment to cybersecurity is determined by its income level, with a correlation coefficient to GDP per capita of 0.55. In this sense, the countries that are leading in the protection ranking are high-income countries (HICs). However, low-income countries (LICs) show the largest average improvement in GCI score from 2020 to 2024, equal to 24 points, followed by lower-middle-income countries (LMICs) with 17, upper-middle-income countries (UMICs) with 13, and HICs with 4 (see annex 1C).

FIGURE 1B.1 Framework for a country's Cybersecurity Readiness Profile

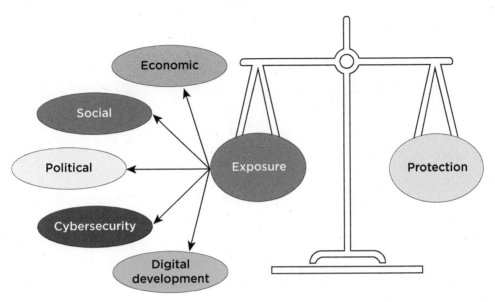

Source: Original figure for this book.

Annex 1C: Bridging the Gap: Variation in Commitment Scores versus Relative Exposure

FIGURE 1C.1 Changes in cybersecurity commitment scores and relative exposure, 2020–24

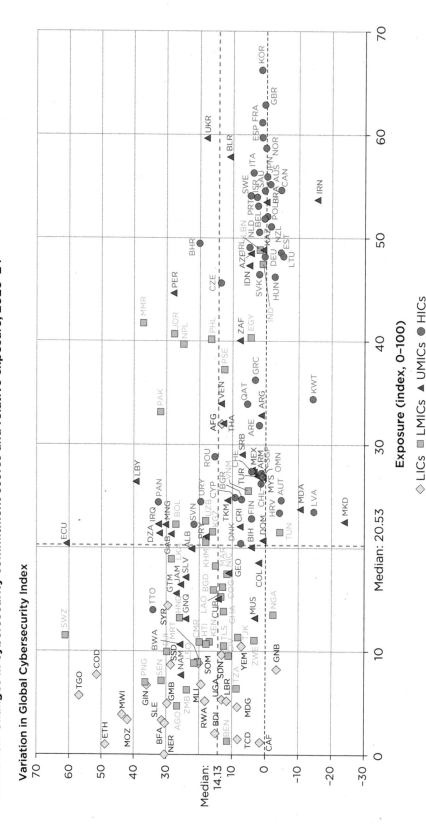

Source: Original figure for this book, based on data from the International Telecommunication Union's Global Cybersecurity Index (GCI).

Note: The figure excludes the outliers China, the Russian Federation, and the United States. Data for protection (y-axis) reflect the change in the GCI from 2020 to 2024; the years for the data on exposure (x-axis) vary. HICs = high-income countries; LICs = low-income countries; LMICs = lower-middle-income countries; UMICs = upper-middle-income countries. For country abbreviations, see International Organization for Standardization (ISO), https://www.iso.org/obp/ui/#search.

Notes

1. Connected individuals are defined as the population accessing the internet (International Telecommunication Union).

2. Commonly, cyberspace is thought to have three layers: (1) physical, (2) cyber persona, and (3) logical. However, some authors might differ from this approach, including additional components such as a governance layer and a content layer.

3. Throughout, this book refers to non-high-income countries as "developing countries."

4. International Telecommunication Union online statistics show that over this period, the share of connected individuals in developing countries increased from 6.8 to 62.7 percent, while in HICs, it increased from 57.9 to 93.2 percent.

5. From 2005 to 2023, the number of individuals using the internet in HICs increased from 654 million to 1.16 billion, while the number in developing countries increased from 368 million to 4.25 billion.

6. The 2024 Global Cybersecurity Index score measures countries' commitments to cybersecurity at the global level. Each country's level of development or engagement in cybersecurity is assessed along five pillars: (1) legal measures, (2) technical measures, (3) organizational measures, (4) capacity development, and (5) cooperation. These are aggregated into an overall score.

7. Annex 1A provides additional information on the data used in this analysis.

8. Measures of political stability can be found in the Worldwide Governance Indicators database, www.govindicators.org.

9. A limitation of the data is that it only includes publicly disclosed cyber incidents, which could bias the distribution between politically and financially motivated cyber incidents.

10. Appgate's "Fraud Beat Annual Report" for 2023 also places LAC as the region with the highest growth rate of cyber incidents, with a 60 percent increase from 2022 to 2023. See https://www.appgate.com/resources/ebooks/fraud-beat-annual-report.

11. International Telecommunication Union statistics.

12. https://www.eleconomista.com.mx/empresas/El-rescate-por-el-hackeo-a-Pemex-es-el -segundo-mayor-por-ransomware-20191115-0035.html.

13. https://www.cnn.com/2019/09/17/americas/ecuador-data-leak-intl-hnk-scli/index.html.

14. https://www.elmostrador.cl/destacado/2020/09/07/el-lunes-negro-de-banco-estado -gobierno-admite-ataque-cibernetico-muy-profundo-y-la-fiscalia-inicia-investigaciones -con-la-pdi/.

15. This taxonomy of cyber incidents is based on Harry and Gallagher (2018).

16. https://www.cyber.gc.ca/sites/default/files/cyber-threats-canada-democratic-process -2023-update-v1-e.pdf.

17. https://www.resecurity.com/blog/article/global-malicious-activity-targeting-elections -is-skyrocketing.

18. The classification of industries and sectors used in this book follows the North American Industry Classification System, which is a hierarchical classification system commonly used by US organizations to collect and analyze information on the economy. "Utilities"

contains three main categories: (1) electric power generation, transmission, and distribution; (2) natural gas distribution; and (3) water, sewerage, and other systems.

19. In the United States, banks are mandated to disclose cyber incidents to various regulatory authorities, such as the Federal Reserve System, the Office of the Comptroller of the Currency, the Federal Deposit Insurance Corporation, and the Consumer Financial Protection Bureau.

20. Specialized computer emergency response teams offer bank information security audit services.

21. https://www.nytimes.com/paidpost/us-bank/what-banks-are-doing-to-protect -customers.html.

22. Examples include compliance with the 1999 Gramm-Leach-Bliley Act, which contributes to the cybersecurity of the sector by maintaining comprehensive privacy policies and practices to safeguard the confidentiality of customer information. Additionally, organizations that handle credit cards are subject to the Payment Card Industry Data Security Standard, which sets guidelines for secure data storage. Perhaps the most important of all is the Federal Reserve Act itself, which grants the Federal Reserve System (the Fed) regulatory authority over banks and financial institutions in the United States. Although the Act does not specifically address cybersecurity, it provides the Fed broad supervisory and regulatory powers over the sector.

23. The Federal Deposit Insurance Corporation, https://www.fdic.gov/regulations /examinations/supervisory/insights/siwin06/siwinter2006-article01.html.

24. Banks based in North America also stand out in terms of their use of cyber insurance, with 91 percent implementing a standalone policy (https://www.cybersecuritydive.com /news/banks-cyber-security-investments/610045/).

25. https://www.prnewswire.com/news-releases/treasury-prime-announces-partnership -with-effectiv-to-bring-fraud-detection-to-enterprises-and-banks-302002806.html.

26. These results come from using a cross-country Poisson regression analysis model to show a potential association between the number of disclosed cyber incidents and different factors, like the employment rate, internet users, internet quality, corruption levels, political stability, and income group, among others. The model implies that the number of disclosed cyber incidents = $\exp(X\beta)$, with X being a vector of the factors that are potentially correlated with the number of disclosed cyber incidents, using data in 2022 for 85 countries. The results show how the political environment of a country could potentially help to predict the incidence rate of cyber incidents. The government indicators used in this model were measured relative to the base group. The base group for the level of corruption is high-level corruption; the one for government effectiveness is low government effectiveness; and the one for the political stability is low political stability.

27. According to Woods and Böhme (2021), surface exposure entails factors that increase potential vectors of compromise.

28. The variables included in the Cybersecurity Readiness Profile are drawn from international institutions like GSMA Intelligence, the ITU, Ookla, World Development Indicators, International Monetary Fund, Center for Strategic and International Studies

at Maryland, and the World Bank, among others; web scraping of disclosed cyber incidents; industry reports; existing cybersecurity indexes; and other sources. Some of the variables are from other well-known indexes, such as the National Cyber Security Index Digital Development Level 2023. For more information, see annex 1B.

29. The topics of data unavailability and data integrity in cybersecurity are discussed by Anderson et al. (2013), Chen et al. (2023), and Kigerl (2016), among others.

30. For example, India has one of the strictest reporting rules in the world, which states that there is a six-hour reporting window in the event of a major cyber incident.

31. Examples of literature studying the United States include Akey et al. (2021); Amir, Levi, and Livne (2018); Kamiya et al. (2021); Lending, Minnick, and Schorno (2018); Lin et al. (2020); Piccotti and Wang (2022); and Tosun (2021).

32. The importance of finding evidence on the impact of cybersecurity capacity building is discussed by Dutton et al. (2019) and Shillair et al. (2022).

33. For example, in Odisha, India, a cyclone in 1999 caused 10,000 fatalities, prompting the government to invest in early warning systems, which paid off—when a similar cyclone struck in 2013, the number of fatalities was reduced to 38 as people could be evacuated in time.

34. Cyberattack surface or potential infiltration points for malicious entities.

References

Akey, P., S. Lewellen, I. Liskovich, and C. Schiller. 2021. "Hacking Corporate Reputations." Working Paper 3143740, Rotman School of Management, University of Toronto, Ontario, Canada.

Al Qartah, A. 2020. "Evolving Ransomware Attacks on Healthcare Providers." Master's thesis, Utica College, Utica, NY.

Amir, E., S. Levi, and T. Livne. 2018. "Do Firms Underreport Information on Cyber-Attacks? Evidence from Capital Markets." *Review of Accounting Studies* 23: 1177–206.

Anderson, R., C. Barton, R. Böhme, R. Clayton, M. J. Van Eeten, M. Levi, T. Moore, and S. Savage. 2013. "Measuring the Cost of Cybercrime." In *The Economics of Information Security and Privacy*, edited by R. Böhme, 265–300. Springer.

Asal, V., J. Mauslein, A. Murdie, J. Young, K. Cousins, and C. Bronk. 2016. "Repression, Education, and Politically Motivated Cyberattacks." *Journal of Global Security Studies* 1 (3): 235–47.

Brando, D., A. Kotidis, A. Kovner, M. Lee, and S. L. Schreft. 2022. "Implications of Cyber Risk for Financial Stability." *FEDS Notes*, Board of Governors of the Federal Reserve System, Washington, DC.

Case, D. U. 2016. "Analysis of the Cyber Attack on the Ukrainian Power Grid." Electricity Information Sharing and Analysis Center, Washington, DC.

Chen, S., M. Hao, F. Ding, D. Jiang, J. Dong, S. Zhang, Q. Guo, and C. Gao. 2023. "Exploring the Global Geography of Cybercrime and Its Driving Forces." *Humanities and Social Sciences Communications* 10 (1): 1–10.

Clinton, L. 2023. *Fixing American Cybersecurity: Creating a Strategic Public-Private Partnership*. Washington, DC: Georgetown University Press.

Dutton, W. H., S. Creese, R. Shillair, and M. Bada. 2019. "Cybersecurity Capacity: Does It Matter?" *Journal of Information Policy* 9: 280–306.

The Economist. 2022. "How Ukraine Fends Off Russian Cyber-Warfare." *The Economist*, November 30.

Evans Data Corporation. 2023. "Worldwide Developer Population and Demographic Study." Evans Data Corporation, Santa Cruz, CA. https://evansdata.com/reports/viewRelease .php?reportID=9.

Ghafur, S., S. Kristensen, K. Honeyford, G. Martin, A. Darzi, and P. Aylin. 2019. "A Retrospective Impact Analysis of the WannaCry Cyberattack on the NHS." *npj Digital Medicine* 2: article 98.

Gordon, L. A., and M. P. Loeb. 2002. "The Economics of Information Security Investment." *ACM Transactions on Information and System Security* 5 (4): 438–57.

Hall, T., and U. Ziemer. 2023. "Cybercrime in Commonwealth West Africa and the Regional Cyber-Criminogenic Framework." *Commonwealth Cybercrime Journal* 1 (1): 5–27.

Harry, C., and N. Gallagher. 2018. "Classifying Cyber Events." *Journal of Information Warfare* 17 (3): 17–31.

Howell, C. J., and G. W. Burruss. 2020. "Datasets for Analysis of Cybercrime." In *The Palgrave Handbook of International Cybercrime and Cyberdeviance*, edited by T. J. Holt and A. M. Bossler, 207–19. Springer.

Ikwu, R. 2019. "Identifying Data and Information Streams in Cyberspace: A Multi-Dimensional Perspective." arXiv preprint arXiv:1906.03757.

Kamiya, S., J. K. Kang, J. Kim, A. Milidonis, and R. M. Stulz. 2021. "Risk Management, Firm Reputation, and the Impact of Successful Cyberattacks on Target Firms." *Journal of Financial Economics* 139 (3): 719–49.

Kigerl, A. 2012. "Routine Activity Theory and the Determinants of High Cybercrime Countries." *Social Science Computer Review* 30 (4): 470–86.

Kigerl, A. 2016. "Cyber Crime Nation Typologies: K-Means Clustering of Countries Based on Cyber Crime Rates." *International Journal of Cyber Criminology* 10 (2): 147–69.

Kshetri, N. 2010. *The Global Cybercrime Industry: Economic, Institutional and Strategic Perspectives*. Springer Science+Business Media.

Kshetri, N., and J. F. DeFranco. 2020. "The Economics of Cyberattacks on Brazil." *Computer* 53 (9): 85–90.

Kumar, S., and K. M. Carley. 2016. "Approaches to Understanding the Motivations behind Cyber Attacks." In *2016 IEEE Conference on Intelligence and Security Informatics*, 307–9. Institute of Electrical and Electronics Engineers, Piscataway, NJ.

Lending, C., K. Minnick, and P. J. Schorno. 2018. "Corporate Governance, Social Responsibility, and Data Breaches." *Financial Review* 53 (2): 413–55.

Lin, Z., T. R. Sapp, J. R. Ulmer, and R. Parsa. 2020. "Insider Trading ahead of Cyber Breach Announcements." *Journal of Financial Markets* 50: 100527.

Mester, L. J. 2019. "Cybersecurity and Financial Stability." Speech at the Federal Reserve Bank of Cleveland, Cleveland, OH, November 21.

Mezzour, G., L. Carley, and K. M. Carley. 2014. "Global Mapping of Cyber-Attacks." SSRN 2729302.

OECD (Organisation for Economic Co-operation and Development). 2023. *Digital Government Review of Latin America and the Caribbean: Building Inclusive and Responsive Public Services.* Paris: OECD (accessed April 4, 2024), https://books.google.com/books/about/Digital_Government_Review_of_Latin_Ameri.html?id=0c8o0AEACAAJ.

Onuora, A. C., D. C. Uche, F. O. Ogbunude, and F. O. Uwazuruike. 2017. "The Challenges of Cybercrime in Nigeria: An Overview." *AIPFU Journal of School of Sciences* 1 (2): 6–11.

Overvest, B., and B. Straathof. 2015. "What Drives Cybercrime? Empirical Evidence from DDoS Attacks." No. 306, CPB Netherlands Bureau for Economic Policy Analysis, The Hague, Netherlands.

PCMI (Payments and Commerce Market Intelligence). 2023. "The 2023 Latin America E-commerce Blueprint." PCMI (accessed April 6, 2024), https://paymentscmi.com/wp-content/uploads/2023/08/2023_PCMI_Blueprint_Standard_August-2023.pdf.

Pérez Colón, R., S. Navajas, and E. Terry. 2019. *IoT in LAC 2019: Taking the Pulse of the Internet of Things in Latin America and the Caribbean.* Washington, DC: Inter-American Development Bank.

Piccotti, L. R., and H. Wang. 2022. "Informed Trading in the Options Market Surrounding Data Breaches." *Global Finance Journal* 56: 100774.

Shillair, R., P. Esteve-González, W. H. Dutton, S. Creese, E. Nagyfejeo, and B. von Solms. 2022. "Cybersecurity Education, Awareness Raising, and Training Initiatives: National Level Evidence-Based Results, Challenges, and Promise." *Computers & Security* 119: 10.

Tosun, O. K. 2021. "Cyber-Attacks and Stock Market Activity." *International Review of Financial Analysis* 76: 101795.

Transforma Insights. 2024. "Current IoT Forecast Highlights." Transforma Insights, Reading, UK (accessed January 19, 2024), https://transformainsights.com/research/forecast/highlights.

Trend Micro. 2023. "Trend Micro 2023 Midyear Cybersecurity Threat Report." Trend Micro, Tokyo (accessed April 4, 2024), https://www.trendmicro.com/vinfo/us/security/research-and-analysis/threat-reports/roundup/stepping-ahead-of-risk-trend-micro-2023-midyear-cybersecurity-threat-report.

Vergara Cobos, E., S. Cakir, H. Mei-Zahav, and B. Barakcin. Forthcoming. "The Role of Cybersecurity in Economic Performance." Working Paper, World Bank, Washington, DC.

Vergara Cobos, E., and E. Malásquez. 2023. "Growth and Transformative Effects of ICT Adoption: A Survey." Policy Research Working Paper 10352, World Bank, Washington, DC.

Votipka, D., K. R. Fulton, J. Parker, M. Hou, M. L. Mazurek, and M. Hicks. 2020. "Understanding Security Mistakes Developers Make: Qualitative Analysis from Build It, Break It, Fix It." In *29th USENIX Security Symposium* (USENIX Security 20), 109–26. Berkeley, CA: USENIX.

Woods, D. W., and R. Böhme. 2021. "SoK: Quantifying Cyber Risk." In *2021 IEEE Symposium on Security and Privacy*, 211–28. Piscataway, NJ: Institute of Electrical and Electronics Engineers.

CHAPTER 2

The Economic Costs of Cyber Incidents

Key Messages

- Cybersecurity is critical for the inclusive and sustainable growth of nations. Estimates suggest that a developing country that reduces its cyber incidents from the top to the bottom quartile of the distribution could see a 1.5 percent increase in gross domestic product (GDP) per capita.

- Cyber incidents can impact the macroeconomic stability of nations, with one major cyber incident having resulted in losses of up to 2.4 percent of the targeted country's GDP.

- With lower cybersecurity commitments and resilience, a rise in cyber incidents could lead to a greater economic impact in developing countries than in high-income countries (HICs).

- Over 40 percent of cyber incidents may remain undisclosed, suggesting that the observed losses from cyber incidents could be just the tip of the iceberg.

- From 2014 to 2021, industries with higher exposure to cyber incidents performed better in countries that had higher initial levels of cybersecurity commitments, all else equal.

- The average unit and aggregate costs of cyber incidents show increasing trajectories, especially since the COVID-19 pandemic, across the health care and financial sectors and among small and medium enterprises.

- The economic toll of cyber incidents is driven mainly by indirect losses that often exceed the direct financial losses faced by victims.

- The sectors that exhibit the largest indirect costs are the most financially, technically, and operationally interconnected, while the sectors more at risk of cyber incidents are those that handle highly confidential consumer data, supply critical social services, and have significant financial assets.

- Cyber runs have been prevented thanks to banks' proactive planning and efficient regulators.
- Empirical evidence shows that following a cyber incident, various effects can occur, including:
  - Increased cash flow retention
  - Decreased shareholder wealth
  - Reduction in corporate bondholders
  - Short selling
  - Negative stock market returns and decreased stock prices
  - Reduction in research and development investment
  - Supply chain disruptions
  - Economic losses for consumers of targeted firms
  - Drops in sales that can last for up to three years after the incident
  - Propagation of losses through supply chains
  - Disruption of national trade flows
  - Erosion of firms' reputations
  - Erosion of consumer trust in the digital economy.

Introduction

Cyber incidents can have profound impacts on economies, with cases like Costa Rica's 2022 ransomware attack, which represented losses of nearly 2.4 percent of the country's gross domestic product (GDP). The effects are not limited to the financial losses faced by victims, but often extend to costs within networks of interconnected economic systems. Moreover, cyber incidents are also endangering human safety. For example, the disruptions from the 2017 NotPetya cyberattack resulted in consumer losses that were four times greater than the losses faced by the directly affected firms, as well as significant risks to patient care, given the inclusion of hospitals and other medical facilities among the affected organizations (Crosignani, Macchiavelli, and Silva 2023).

Examination of the economic ramifications of cyber incidents reveals a landscape that is fraught with challenges yet full of opportunities for understanding and fortifying against future threats. This chapter underscores the multifaceted dimensions of the economic impacts of cyber incidents and the urgency of taking proactive measures to mitigate their far-reaching consequences.

The literature proves that cyber incidents can lead to economic losses through reputational damage, instability in capital markets, supply chain disruptions, erosion of trust, and disincentives to invest, among other channels. However, it is worth noting that there is a large bias in the study of cybersecurity toward high-income countries, with over 90 percent of the literature focusing only on the United States. The centralization of research stems from the limited data available to conduct empirical studies and a lack of support for cybersecurity research and development (R&D). Therefore, there could be unexplored channels through which cyber incidents impact the economy in the context of developing countries.

The economic ramifications of cyber incidents are projected to continue to escalate, especially in developing countries; for the most vulnerable, such as small and medium enterprises (SMEs); and in highly interconnected sectors. However, research shows that in the digital age, higher levels of national cybersecurity commitments may not only help to protect systems, but also boost the economic performance of industries, especially the more digitalized ones.

This chapter presents new and existing literature on the economic costs of cyber incidents. It also discusses the cost trends, types of costs, and the overall link between economic outputs and cyber incidents, and cybersecurity. The chapter concludes with policy recommendations aimed at strategically minimizing the costliest effects of cyber incidents.

Cybersecurity and Macroeconomic Stability

Managing cyber risk and minimizing major cyber incidents are important for promoting inclusive and sustainable development, as well as fostering economic growth. According to Vergara Cobos et al. (forthcoming), if a developing country cuts its number of major reported cyber incidents from the highest to the lowest quartile in the distribution—roughly decreasing from 50 to 7 incidents within a decade—it could achieve a 1.5 percent increase in GDP per capita. In this context, as cyber incidents pose a macroeconomic threat to countries (IMF 2024), efficient cybersecurity could foster economic growth.

Although various sources have tried to estimate the global GDP losses from cyber incidents, the presence and range of indirect costs make it challenging to produce a confident assessment. Moreover, with probably over 40 percent of cyber incidents unreported, the challenge of costing cyber incidents is even bigger. Nevertheless, research suggests that disclosed cyber incidents are statistically significantly negatively correlated with economic growth, especially among developing countries (Vergara Cobos et al., forthcoming).[1]

Additionally, national-level cybersecurity commitments could be playing an important role in the performance of digitalized industries. Controlling for country and industry fixed effects, as well as possible endogeneity issues and confounding factors, new research suggests that industries that experienced a relatively higher level of exposure to cyber incidents (for example, wholesale, hospitality, utilities, and manufacturing, as opposed to construction and agriculture) had higher residual growth rates from 2014 to 2021 in countries with higher initial levels of cybersecurity commitments (measured by the 2014 Global Cybersecurity Index [GCI] score), all else equal (Vergara Cobos et al., forthcoming).[2]

Table 2.1 contrasts the impact of cybersecurity commitments on the growth rates across various industrial sectors, stratified by countries with GCI scores below and above the median. The table shows the average residual growth rates of real value added from 2014 to 2021, after accounting for industry and country-specific effects. For example, for industries that are more exposed to cyber incidents, the residual growth rates in countries with lower scores for cybersecurity commitments are in the negative range, with manufacturing exhibiting the most significant drop of around −0.8 percent. In countries with higher levels of cybersecurity commitments, these sectors show positive residual growth, with manufacturing having the most substantial residual growth rate of approximately 0.7 percent. In the less exposed industries, the pattern is reversed—countries with lower GCI scores show growth rates in construction and agriculture, while in countries with higher GCI scores, these industries present negative growth rates.

Trends and Cost Characteristics of Cyber Incidents

Consistent with the increasing frequency of disclosed cyber incidents, discussed in chapter 1, the literature published between 2017 and 2023 on the aggregate costs of cyber incidents sheds light on the escalating trajectory of losses due to cyber incidents across various countries and regions, and at the global level.

TABLE 2.1 Effect of cybersecurity commitments on the growth rate of real gross value added, by industry, 2014–21

Sector	Countries with below-median GCI scores (growth rate, %)	Countries with above-median GCI scores (growth rate, %)
Industries most often subject to cyberattacks		
Wholesale, retail trade, restaurants, and hotels (ISIC G–H)	−0.04059	0.03146
Mining, quarrying, and utilities (ISIC C–E)	−0.30133	0.25937
Transport, storage, and communication (ISIC I)	−0.70363	0.58349
Manufacturing (ISIC D)	−0.85575	0.71493
Industries least often subject to cyberattacks		
Construction (ISIC F)	0.45236	−0.39914
Agriculture, hunting, forestry, and fishing (ISIC A–B)	1.41115	−1.35395

Source: Vergara Cobos et al., forthcoming.
Note: The table reports the average residual compound growth rate of real value added between 2014 and 2021, which was obtained after controlling for industry and country fixed effects. GCI = Global Cybersecurity Index; ISIC = International Standard Industrial Classification of All Economic Activities.

However, as the frequency and types of cyber incidents vary worldwide, so does the aggregate cost, which is estimated to be higher among high-income countries but increasing in developing countries, especially considering their lower levels of cybersecurity commitments (Świątkowska 2020).

For example, in Africa, the financial consequences of small- and medium-scale cyber incidents could be substantial, especially given the rapid digitalization across the continent that gives rise to new and costlier types of cyber threats. By 2024, Africans are experiencing a steady rise in online scams (facilitated by the new social media phishing), ransomware (via traditional or email phishing), and digital extortion that employs a constantly evolving set of techniques (Interpol 2024). This situation could result in significant losses across the continent.[3]

The challenging scenario of the increasing number of cyber incidents is accompanied by a steadily rising unit cost across various types of attacks. IBM (2024) reports that the average cost of a data breach has risen by 10 percent in

2024 compared to 2023, reaching about US$4.88 million, the highest total ever recorded (figure 2.1). The rise in unit costs has been particularly significant for SMEs, especially since the COVID-19 pandemic. For example, for organizations with fewer than 500 employees, the average cost of a data breach surged by 13.4 percent between 2022 and 2023, but those with 10,000 to 25,000 employees reported a decrease of 1.8 percent, and those with more than 25,000 employees saw a drop of 2.5 percent in the same period (IBM 2023).

FIGURE 2.1 Global average cost of a data breach, 2017–24

Average cost (US$, millions)

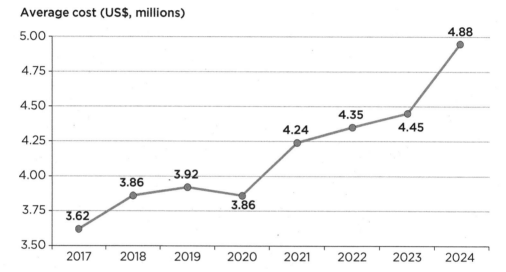

Source: Original figure for this book, based on data from IBM (2023, 2024).

Across sectors, costlier data breaches are observed in health care and finance (figure 2.2), which are two of the most attacked sectors across developing countries. Such findings indicate that the cost of a data breach is a function of three main aspects:

• The confidentiality of the compromised data

• The criticality of the services at risk of disruption

• The financial assets of the targeted victim.

FIGURE 2.2 Cost of a data breach, by sector, 2022 and 2023

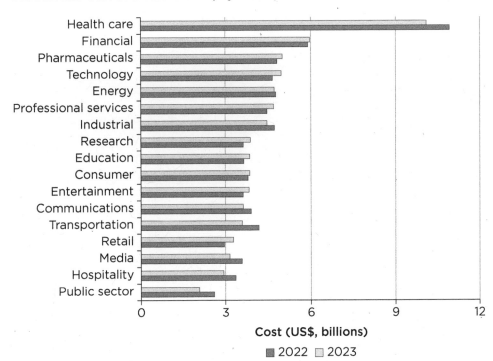

Cost (US$, billions)

■ 2022 □ 2023

Source: Original figure for this book, based on data from IBM 2023.
Note: The data are for 553 organizations of various sizes across 16 countries and 17 industries.

The Challenge of Measuring Indirect Costs

Indirect costs from cyber incidents refer to the secondary losses that extend beyond the immediate financial losses faced by victims. These costs can be substantial and multifaceted, affecting various aspects of businesses, consumers, and the broader economy (figure 2.3). The critical distinction between direct and indirect costs lies in the exponential growth potential of the latter compared to the eventual limit of direct losses. This dynamic poses disproportionate societal burdens and raises concerns about the efficacy of efforts to combat cyber incidents (Anderson et al. 2013).

Notable indirect costs are related to:

- *Changes in consumer behavior.* Targeted firms could experience a drop in sales for up to three years after the incident, caused by a change in consumers' risk perception (Kamiya et al. 2021).

FIGURE 2.3 Types of costs originating from cyber incidents

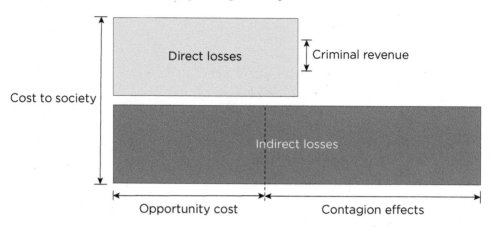

Source: Original figure for this book, based on Anderson et al. 2013.
Note: This book's framework assumes that indirect losses encompass a set of opportunity costs faced by the targeted organization and the losses from contagion effects such as the costs faced by consumers and shareholders, as well as other second- and third-round effects. Under Anderson et al.'s (2013) framework, the social costs of cyber incidents include direct or explicit costs, such as the monetary value of the victim's loss due to a cyberattack, including the criminal revenue; indirect or implicit costs, which are defined as the opportunity costs of a breach, for example, the economic costs created by the loss of trust in the victim; and defense or prevention costs, which include the costs of development, deployment, and maintenance of a secure cyberspace, such as spam filters, and which could also be seen as investments.

- *Reputational harm.* Large data breaches are associated with a loss of 5 to 9 percent of intangible reputational capital (Makridis 2021).

- *Capital market reactions.* Abnormal levels of trading activity have been observed in the United States, suggesting that there is short selling exploiting insider knowledge of cyber incidents (Wang et al. 2022). Research on the United States also shows that firms' immediate disclosure of a cyber incident resulted in a 0.3 percent average decline in equity values over three days and a 0.72 percent decline over a month. Conversely, when attacks were not disclosed and were later discovered externally, the decline was much steeper: 1.5 percent over three days and 3.56 percent over a month (Amir, Levi, and Livne 2018). Similarly, cyber incidents impact bondholder wealth, with research showing that bondholders lost approximately 2 percent of wealth within one month after the incident. However, unlike stocks, bonds do not react to cyber incidents in the short term (Iyer, Simkins, and Wang 2020).

- *Response costs.* Firms try to compensate for the erosion of their reputation by investing more in corporate social responsibility and increasing their cash holdings (Akey et al. 2021).

- *Contagion effects.* Cyber risks propagate between firms and escalate from the firm to the sectoral level (Jamilov, Rey, and Tahoun 2021), with suppliers and unaffected peer firms reacting in similar ways as the directly hit firms, for example, by also increasing cash holdings following a cyber incident (Garg 2020). Moreover, indirect costs can propagate across an entire industry, for example, by altering investors' perception of the risk distribution in the industry (Kamiya et al. 2021).

Cyber incidents can lead to contagion effects or the propagation of second- and third-round effects. This was seen during the 2017 NotPetya cyberattack, which is estimated to have caused financial losses of more than US$7.3 billion for customers of the affected firms, almost four times the initial decline in profits reported by the directly impacted firms (Crosignani, Macchiavelli, and Silva 2023). The main issue of seeing contagion effects—also known in the cybersecurity field as "cascading failures"—lies in the financial sector, where the term was coined. Cyber runs, or scenarios often triggered by cyber incidents that lead to a widespread loss of confidence in the security and reliability of the financial system, are similar to bank runs in that they have the potential to cause rapid financial and operational instability, representing a great risk for economies worldwide. Although a cyber run has not materialized, the systemic nature of modern financial systems implies that a cyber incident can have far-reaching consequences, unless proactive measures to avoid multiple rounds of effects are put in place. For example, in 2019, a multiday cyberattack on a US technology service provider used by banks impaired the ability of its customers to send payments, which left other banks with fewer resources and at risk of failing to send their own payments. In that case, the precautionary actions taken by the secondarily affected banks, including contingency planning, as well as the availability of liquidity buffers and the support of the Federal Reserve prevented the crisis from causing third- or fourth-round effects or even a cyber run (Kotidis and Schreft 2022).

On the reactions of capital markets, research also shows that cyber risk is factored into equity prices, which means that companies with elevated cyber risk exhibit superior performance during normal periods yet encounter significant declines after the revelation of a cybersecurity breach (Florackis et al. 2023). Capital markets can react even before the announcement of a cyber incident, with evidence showing that informed insiders and hackers engage in opportunistic short selling before the announcement, which further debilitates the stability of the markets (Garg 2020; Lin et al. 2020; Piccotti and Wang 2022). However, responses to announcements of cybersecurity breaches vary based on the characteristics of the incident, with compromises in confidentiality and functionality being the most prominent factors. Severe declines in the stock market values of compromised firms occur if the incident involves customer records rather than employee records, especially when the incident involves highly confidential data (Akey et al. 2021; Campbell et al. 2003). In terms of operations, firms experiencing function-related failures see a greater drop in market value (1.48 percent) compared to firms with data-related failures (0.75 percent) (Goldstein, Chernobai, and Benaroch 2011), especially if the incident is a denial-of-service attack (Garg, Curtis, and Halper 2003).

Victims often adjust their behavior to counteract the damage to their reputation, leading to positive preventive measures but greater short-term costs. Many targeted firms, as well as their suppliers and unaffected peers, increase investment in corporate social responsibility, typically by 0.4 to 0.5 standard deviations, to mitigate the reputational losses incurred (Akey et al. 2021); exhibit a higher likelihood of replacing their chief executive officer and chief technology officer; make greater efforts to enhance their social responsibility practices (Lending, Minnick, and Schorno 2018); and invest more in R&D (Garg 2020; Tosun 2021).

Policy Recommendations

The economic toll of cyber incidents extends beyond the direct financial losses and encompasses revenue reductions, decreased consumer trust, decreased investment in R&D, trade disruptions, and more, culminating in an overall economic impact that could lead to macroeconomic vulnerability for nations. The analysis presented in this chapter supports the following policy recommendations for developing countries:

1. *Enhance national cybersecurity commitments to stimulate growth* in the most targeted and digitalized industries, like information and communications.

2. *Monitor the digitalization of the health care sector* and implement cybersecurity measures concurrently with digital advancements.

3. *Prioritize highly attractive sectors* handling highly confidential consumer data, critical social services, and significant financial assets. These are prime targets for cyber attackers seeking financial gains.

4. *Give precedence to cybersecurity in e-government initiatives,* as incidents frequently occur in the public sector in developing countries and can lead to above-average economic losses.

5. *Remain vigilant in detecting potential cyber runs*[4] and undertake proactive actions such as contingency planning, liquidity buffers, and preparedness of a strong financial regulator that can monitor the soundness of the financial sector and act in response to contagion threats.

6. *Consider sectors' interconnectedness.* Evaluate the potential economic impacts of cyber incidents based on sectors' levels of financial and technological interconnectedness.

7. *Promote inclusive cybersecurity research and data collection efforts* to understand the diverse economic implications of cyber incidents across industries and nations. Increasing funding and support for research in developing countries will provide valuable insights into the unique challenges and opportunities associated with cybersecurity in these contexts.

8. *Monitor indirect short- and long-term losses.* Cyber incidents are linked to both short-term (for example, instability in the capital markets) and long-term (for example, disruptions in value chains) economic losses. Therefore, governments must establish postincident monitoring measures of negative economic effects, which may occur even years after an incident occurs.

9. *Ensure that cybersecurity regulatory measures protect economic stability* and protect the victims of cyber incidents from indirect losses.

10. *Encourage cyber audits,* especially in critical sectors, for the proactive identification of important vulnerabilities.

11. *Promote safe reporting of cyber incidents* that considers the indirect losses related to the announcement of cyber incidents.

Annex 2A: Aggregated Costs of Cyber Incidents

Aggregated estimates of the annual global cost of cyber incidents are limited, and among those available, there are substantive methodological gaps (table 2A.1).

TABLE 2A.1 **Aggregated estimates of the annual global cost of all cyber incidents**

Source	Methodology	Data	Aggregated global annual cost estimate (US$, billions)	Share of global GDP (%)
IC3 (2017)	Unavailable	Complaints received by the IC3	1.42	0.0018
Norton (2017)	Online survey with 21,539 individuals ages 18+ across 20 countries	Captures only the losses of consumers	172	0.21
McAfee and CSIS (2018)	Compiles from literature the direct and indirect loss estimates for many countries and aggregates them using an unavailable methodology	Data subject to measurement error	522.5	0.6
Cybersecurity Ventures (2019)	Unavailable	Estimates based on historical cybercrime rates	6,000	6.9
IC3 (2019)	Unavailable	Complaints received by the IC3	2.71	0.003
IC3 (2020)	Unavailable	Complaints received by the IC3	3.50	0.004
European Commission (2019) estimate for 2020	Unavailable	Data source not available	6,070	7.1
eSentire and Cybersecurity Ventures (2022)	Unavailable	Estimates based on historical cybercrime rates	8,000 (2023 projection)	8
eSentire and Cybersecurity Ventures (2022)	Unavailable	Estimates based on historical cybercrime rates	10,500 (2025 projection)	9.1

Source: Original table for this book.
Note: These aggregated estimates do not differentiate the severity or type of cyber incident. The methodologies used to estimate these findings have not been validated by the author of this chapter. The source for global nominal GDP (in US$) is the International Monetary Fund. GDP = gross domestic product; IC3 = Internet Crime Complaint Center.

Similarly, country-level cost estimates across regions exist but are rare. According to the UK Cabinet Office, in 2011, the UK government estimated that the cost of cybercrime was US$33.67 billion, or about 1.3 percent of the country's gross domestic product (GDP), with the largest share posed to businesses—about 78 percent. Similarly, in a dramatic increase from a 2014 projection of US$700 million, the total cost of cybercrime in Ireland was estimated to have reached US$10.5 billion in 2020, or 2.5 percent of the country's GDP (Grant Thornton 2021). In contrast, in Latin America and the Caribbean, the cost to the largest targeted country, Brazil, was estimated to be around US$8 billion in 2015, or about 0.4 percent of the country's GDP.[5] Cost estimates provided by McAfee and CSIS (2018) suggest that Europe and Central Asia and East Asia and Pacific could be the leading regions in terms of cybercrime costs (table 2A.2).

TABLE 2A.2 **Regional distribution of cybercrime costs, 2017**

Region	Region GDP (US$, trillions)	Cybercrime cost (US$, billions)	Cybercrime loss (% of GDP)
North America	20.2	140–175	0.69–0.87
Europe and Central Asia	20.3	160–180	0.79–0.89
East Asia and Pacific	22.5	120–200	0.53–0.89
South Asia	2.9	7–15	0.24–0.52
Latin America and the Caribbean	5.3	15–30	0.28–0.57
Sub-Saharan Africa	1.5	1–3	0.07–0.20
Middle East and North Africa	3.1	2–5	0.06–0.16
World	**75.8**	**445–608**	**0.59–0.80**

Source: McAfee and CSIS 2018.
Note: GDP = gross domestic product.

Annex 2B: Literature Review on the Direct and Indirect Costs of Cyber Incidents

TABLE 2B.1 **Summary of the stock market effects of cyber incidents**

Source	Main finding	Cybersecurity breach/risk data set	Sample	Time coverage
Positive or neutral effects				
Garg (2020)	Firms hold more cash after having a cyberattack. Their suppliers and peer firms also increase their cash holdings.	PRC	United States	2005–17
Bose and Leung (2013)	The announcement of employing identity theft countermeasures is associated with a 0.63 percent increase in a firm's market value.	Construct own data set from news databases	United States	1995–2012
Akey et al. (2021)	Firms compensate for the erosion of their reputation following a data breach by investing 0.4 to 0.5 standard deviation more in corporate social responsibility.	PRC	United States	2005–16
Kannan, Rees, and Sridhar (2007)	There are no significant negative market returns to information security breach announcements.	Construct own data set from news databases	United States	1997–2003
Negative effects				
Wang et al. (2022)	Prior to breach announcements, attacked firms have a 6.8 percent higher Daily Cost of Borrow Score, 0.27 percent higher loan fees, and 0.3 percent lower rebate fees. The abnormal level of trading activity suggests that short sellers exploit insider knowledge of breaches.	PRC	United States	2005–18
Amir, Levi, and Livne (2018)	Managers disclose information on cyberattacks when investors already suspect a high probability of an attack. Withheld (disclosed) cyberattacks are associated with a 2.6 percent (0.7 percent) decrease in equity values.	1. Audit Analytics 2. VERIS Community Database	United States	2010–15

(Continued)

TABLE 2B.1 Summary of the stock market effects of cyber incidents *(continued)*

Source	Main finding	Cybersecurity breach/risk data set	Sample	Time coverage
Negative effects *(continued)*				
Goldstein, Chernobai, and Benaroch (2011)	The market value of firms that have function-related failures drops more (1.48 percent) compared to firms that have data-related events (0.75 percent).	FIRST	United States	1985–2009
Makridis (2021)	Large (small) data breaches are associated with a loss (gain) of 5 to 9 percent (26 to 29 percent) of intangible reputational capital.	PRC	United States	2002–18
Iyer, Simkins, and Wang (2020)	Following a data breach announcement, corporate bondholders have 2 percent negative returns in a month.	PRC	United States	2005–16
Akey et al. (2021)	Firms that announce a breach have a 1.5 to 1.9 percent reduction in cumulative abnormal returns in 30 days. Firms with higher pre-event investment in corporate social responsibility do not lose as much.	PRC	United States	2005–16
Kamiya et al. (2021)	Disclosure of a cyberattack significantly reduces shareholder wealth and sales growth, especially for large firms in the retail industry. Drops in sales can last for three years after the incident. Shareholder wealth decreases by 1.09 percent within three days after an attack announcement.	PRC	United States	2005–17
Garg, Curtis, and Halper (2003)	All types of information technology security breaches yield negative market returns. The market reacts especially to credit card information theft (9 to 15 percent) and denial-of-service incidents (1 to 4 percent).	Construct own data set from news databases	United States	1996–2002

(Continued)

TABLE 2B.1 Summary of the stock market effects of cyber incidents *(continued)*

Source	Main finding	Cybersecurity breach/risk data set	Sample	Time coverage
Negative effects *(continued)*				
Hovav and D'Arcy (2003)	Following a denial-of-service attack, companies that rely on their websites for their business operations have negative stock market returns, while noninternet-specific companies do not experience any reactions.	Construct own data set from news databases	United States	1998–2002
Lending, Minnick, and Schorno (2018)	Firms have a 1.4 percent reduction in returns within three days of a breach announcement. Moreover, attacked firms experience a 3.5 percent reduction in one-year buy-and-hold abnormal returns. Firms with larger boards and boards with less financial expertise are more likely to be targets, while socially responsible firms are less likely to be targets. Firms that improve their governance and social capital following a breach reduce the likelihood of a further breach by 5.03 to 6.78 percent.	PRC	United States	2004–12
Piccotti and Wang (2022)	Transactions in the options market indicate that hackers (insiders) initiate informed trading 12 (four) months before data breach announcements. On average, cumulative abnormal returns of breached firms decrease by 0.46 percent following a breach within five days.	PRC	United States	2005–18
Lin et al. (2020)	Insiders save an average of US$35,000 due to short selling. Following a data breach announcement, stock prices decrease by 1.18 percent in a three-day window, 1.44 percent in a five-day window, 1.26 percent in a 21-day window, and 1.44 percent in a 41-day window.	PRC	United States	2011–16

(Continued)

TABLE 2B.1 Summary of the stock market effects of cyber incidents *(continued)*

Source	Main finding	Cybersecurity breach/risk data set	Sample	Time coverage
Negative effects *(continued)*				
Campbell et al. (2003)	Cumulative abnormal returns of firms decrease by 1.8 percent following a breach announcement involving unauthorized access to confidential data.	Construct own data set from news databases	United States	1996–2000
Tosun (2021)	A cyberattack has a significant negative effect on a firm's stock market value and trading in the short term. Although a cyberattack has no long-run effects on a firm's market value, an impacted firm changes its policies in the long run.	PRC	United States	2004–19
Cavusoglu, Mishra, and Raghunathan (2004)	On average, firms lose 2.1 percent of their market value within two days of the announcement of a cybersecurity breach.	Construct own data set from news databases	United States	1996–2001
Wang, Kannan, and Ulmer (2013)	Firms that disclose risk-mitigating information in their financial reports are less likely to have a security incident. Once a breach occurs, the market less severely punishes the firms that take precautionary action.	Construct own data set from news databases	United States	1997–2008
Acquisti, Friedman, and Telang (2006)	There is a significantly negative but short-lived stock market effect on privacy breach events.	Construct own data set from news databases	United States	1999–2006
Wang et al. (2022)	Abnormal levels of trading activity before data breach announcements indicate that sellers exploit prior knowledge of data breaches.	PRC	United States	2005–18

Source: Vergara Cobos and Cakir, forthcoming.
Note: FIRST = Forum of Incident Response and Security Teams; PRC = Privacy Rights Clearinghouse; VERIS = Vocabulary for Event Recording and Information Sharing.

TABLE 2B.2 Summary of the literature on supply chain effects, systemic risk, and spillover effects of cyber incidents

Source	Main finding	Cybersecurity breach/risk data set	Sample	Time coverage
Crosignani, Macchiavelli, and Silva (2023)	Worldwide suppliers and customers of firms whose operations were halted due to the 2017 NotPetya cyberattack incurred large losses. As a result, directly hit firms had long-lasting reputational damage.	Compiled by the authors	Ukrainian firms hit by NotPetya and their worldwide customers and suppliers	2017–18
Kotidis and Schreft (2022)	A multiday cyberattack on a technology service provider impaired customers' ability to send payments, spilling over to the banks that did not use the technology service provider and leaving them with fewer reserves.	Single event, proprietary data set	United States	n.a.
Corbet and Gurdgiev (2019)	The stock price volatility of a large firm following a data breach announcement creates volatility in both domestic and global markets, especially after 2014.	Construct own data set from news databases	United States	2005–15
Jamilov, Rey, and Tahoun (2021)	Firm-level cyber risk can be a source of systemic risk in financial markets.	Textual analysis of quarterly earnings announcements and question-and-answer sessions	85 countries	2002–21

Source: Vergara Cobos and Cakir, forthcoming.
Note: n.a. = not applicable.

TABLE 2B.3 **Summary of the literature on measuring cybersecurity risk**

Source	Main findings on the risk index	Notes on methods	Sample	Time coverage
Florackis et al. (2023)	Firms with higher risk outperform other firms by up to 8.3 percent per year in terms of equal-weighted (7.9 percent value-weighted) returns.	Textual analysis of annual corporate filings (10,000)	United States	2008–19
Facchinetti, Giudici, and Osmetti (2020)	The riskiest combinations of an attack are those associated with zero-day, phone hacking, and vulnerabilities, in combination with espionage and information warfare.	Theoretical	n.a.	n.a.
Lhuissier and Tripier (2021)	The rise of cybercrime is positively correlated with the performance of cybersecurity companies.	Scraping all tweets worldwide that contain keywords	Global (not broken down by countries)	2011–20
Bouveret (2018)	Cybersecurity threats are growing for financial institutions. Given the reliance of their operations on technology, fintech firms are particularly vulnerable to cyber risks.	Index consists of the number of Factiva articles featuring cybersecurity keywords divided by the number of articles featuring banking keywords like "bank" and "risk," by country	Global (broken down by countries)	2014–17
Keppo and Niemela (2021)	Hacking campaigns increase the target institutions' exposure to the deep web and dark web by 62 percent per year during the first two years after the campaign's start date.	More than 200 million dark web and deep web pages	460 financial institutions in 167 countries targeted by nine ideologically motivated campaigns	2012–18

Source: Vergara Cobos and Cakir, forthcoming.
Note: n.a. = not applicable.

Notes

1. Other estimates cited by the cybersecurity community suggest that the annual global cost of cyber incidents as a share of the world's GDP could be significant (an average of available estimates from 2017 to 2023), although many of these estimates lack a clear methodology for validation (see annex 2A for a full discussion on this).

2. Using a cross-industry, cross-country model with an instrumental variable adaptation, Vergara Cobos et al. (forthcoming) explore how the value added of a given industry in different countries depends on an interaction effect between the home country's cybersecurity commitments and the industry's exposure to cyberattacks. The model assumes that media coverage of cyber incidents, cybersecurity awareness, and reporting are more comprehensive in the United States; thus, it approximates an industry's vulnerability to cyberattacks using the total number of disclosed cyber incidents per industry in the United States during 2017–22. Because the United States is considered the benchmark country, it is excluded from the estimation sample. The model also uses an instrumental variable for controlling confounding factors such as industries' digitalization levels.

3. This is based on estimates made by the Kenyan information technology cybersecurity firm Serianu in 2021 and reported by Interpol (2021).

4. A cyber run is a systemic cyber incident in the financial sector.

5. This estimate was reported by the Security Intelligence website, https://securityintelligence.com/the-true-cost-of-cybercrime-in-brazil/.

References

Acquisti, A., A. Friedman, and R. Telang. 2006. "Is There a Cost to Privacy Breaches? An Event Study." In *Proceedings of the Twenty-Seventh International Conference on Information Systems*, 94. Milwaukee, WI.

Akey, P., S. Lewellen, I. Liskovich, and C. Schiller. 2021. "Hacking Corporate Reputations." Working Paper 3143740, Rotman School of Management, Toronto, Canada.

Amir, E., S. Levi, and T. Livne. 2018. "Do Firms Underreport Information on Cyber-Attacks? Evidence from Capital Markets." *Review of Accounting Studies* 23: 1177–206.

Anderson, R., C. Barton, R. Böhme, R. Clayton, M. J. Van Eeten, M. Levi, T. Moore, and S. Savage. 2013. "Measuring the Cost of Cybercrime." In *The Economics of Information Security and Privacy*, edited by R. Böhme, 265–300. Springer.

Bose, I., and A. C. M. Leung. 2013. "The Impact of Adoption of Identity Theft Countermeasures on Firm Value." *Decision Support Systems* 55 (3): 753–63.

Bouveret, A. 2018. "Cyber Risk for the Financial Sector: A Framework for Quantitative Assessment." IMF Working Paper WP/18/143, International Monetary Fund, Washington, DC.

Campbell, K., L. A. Gordon, M. P. Loeb, and L. Zhou. 2003. "The Economic Cost of Publicly Announced Information Security Breaches: Empirical Evidence from the Stock Market." *Journal of Computer Security* 11 (3): 431–48.

Cavusoglu, H., B. Mishra, and S. Raghunathan. 2004. "The Effect of Internet Security Breach Announcements on Market Value: Capital Market Reactions for Breached Firms and Internet Security Developers." *International Journal of Electronic Commerce* 9 (1): 70–104.

Corbet, S., and C. Gurdgiev. 2019. "What the Hack: Systematic Risk Contagion from Cyber Events." *International Review of Financial Analysis* 65: 101386.

Crosignani, M., M. Macchiavelli, and A. F. Silva. 2023. "Pirates without Borders: The Propagation of Cyberattacks through Firms' Supply Chains." *Journal of Financial Economics* 147 (2): 432–48.

Cybersecurity Ventures. 2019. "2019 Official Annual Cybercrime Report." Cybersecurity Ventures, Herjavec Group, Toronto, Canada.

eSentire and Cybersecurity Ventures. 2022. "2022 Official Cybercrime Report." eSentire, Ontario, Canada. https://s3.ca-central-1.amazonaws.com/esentire-dot-com-assets/assets/resourcefiles/2022-Official-Cybercrime-Report.pdf.

European Commission. 2019. "A Cybersecure Digital Transformation in a Complex Threat Environment." European Commission, Brussels, Belgium. https://digital-strategy.ec.europa.eu/en/library/cybersecure-digital-transformation-complex-threat-environment-brochure.

Facchinetti, S., P. Giudici, and S. A. Osmetti. 2020. "Cyber Risk Measurement with Ordinal Data." *Statistical Methods & Applications* 29 (1): 173–85.

Florackis, C., C. Louca, R. Michaely, and M. Weber. 2023. "Cybersecurity Risk." *Review of Financial Studies* 36 (1): 351–407.

Garg, A., J. Curtis, and H. Halper. 2003. "Quantifying the Financial Impact of IT Security Breaches." *Information Management & Computer Security* 11 (2): 74–83.

Garg, P. 2020. "Cybersecurity Breaches and Cash Holdings: Spillover Effect." *Financial Management* 49 (2): 503–19.

Goldstein, J., A. Chernobai, and M. Benaroch. 2011. "An Event Study Analysis of the Economic Impact of IT Operational Risk and Its Subcategories." *Journal of the Association for Information Systems* 12 (9): 1–23.

Grant Thornton. 2021. "The Economic Cost of Cybercrime." Grant Thornton, San Francisco, CA. https://www.grantthornton.ie/globalassets/1.-member-firms/ireland/insights/publications/grant-thornton---the-economic-cost-of-cybercrime.pdf.

Hovav, A., and J. D'Arcy. 2003. "The Impact of Denial-of-Service Attack Announcements on the Market Value of Firms." *Risk Management and Insurance Review* 6 (2): 97–121.

IBM. 2023. "2023 Cost of a Data Breach." IBM, Armonk, NY.

IBM. 2024. "2024 Cost of a Data Breach." IBM, Armonk, NY.

IC3 (Internet Crime Complaint Center). 2017. "2017 Internet Crime Report." IC3, Federal Bureau of Investigation, Washington, DC.

IC3 (Internet Crime Complaint Center). 2019. "2019 Internet Crime Report." IC3, Federal Bureau of Investigation, Washington, DC.

IC3 (Internet Crime Complaint Center). 2020. "2020 Internet Crime Report." IC3, Federal Bureau of Investigation, Washington, DC.

IMF (International Monetary Fund). 2024. *Global Financial Stability Report*. Washington, DC: IMF.

Interpol. 2021. "African Cyberthreat Assessment Report." Interpol, Lyon, France. https://www.interpol.int/content/download/16759/file/AfricanCyberthreatAssessment_ENGLISH.pdf.

Interpol. 2024. "Interpol African Cyberthreat Assessment Report 2024." Interpol, Lyon, France. https://www.interpol.int/content/download/21048/file/24COM005030-AJFOC_Africa%20Cyberthreat%20Assessment%20Report_2024_complet_EN%20v4.pdf.

Iyer, S. R., B. J. Simkins, and H. Wang. 2020. "Cyberattacks and Impact on Bond Valuation." *Finance Research Letters* 33: 101215.

Jamilov, R., H. Rey, and A. Tahoun. 2021. "The Anatomy of Cyber Risk." Working Paper 28906, National Bureau of Economic Research, Cambridge, MA.

Kamiya, S., J. K. Kang, J. Kim, A. Milidonis, and R. M. Stulz. 2021. "Risk Management, Firm Reputation, and the Impact of Successful Cyberattacks on Target Firms." *Journal of Financial Economics* 139 (3): 719–49.

Kannan, K., J. Rees, and S. Sridhar. 2007. "Market Reactions to Information Security Breach Announcements: An Empirical Analysis." *International Journal of Electronic Commerce* 12 (1): 69–91.

Keppo, J., and M. Niemela. 2021. "Do Hacker Groups Pose a Risk to Organizations? Study on Financial Institutions Targeted by Hacktivists." https://ssrn.com/abstract=3835547 or http://dx.doi.org/10.2139/ssrn.3835547.

Kotidis, A., and S. L. Schreft. 2022. "Cyberattacks and Financial Stability: Evidence from a Natural Experiment." Finance and Economics Discussion Series, Board of Governors of the Federal Reserve System, Washington, DC.

Lending, C., K. Minnick, and P. J. Schorno. 2018. "Corporate Governance, Social Responsibility, and Data Breaches." *Financial Review* 53 (2): 413–55.

Lhuissier, S., and F. Tripier. 2021. "Measuring Cyber Risk." Banque de France, Paris.

Lin, Z., T. R. Sapp, J. R. Ulmer, and R. Parsa. 2020. "Insider Trading ahead of Cyber Breach Announcements." *Journal of Financial Markets* 50: 100527.

Makridis, C. A. 2021. "Do Data Breaches Damage Reputation? Evidence from 45 Companies between 2002 and 2018." *Journal of Cybersecurity* 7 (1): tyab021.

McAfee and CSIS (Center for Strategic and International Studies). 2018. "Economic Impact of Cybercrime Report." McAfee, San Jose, CA (accessed March 29, 2023), https://csis-website-prod.s3.amazonaws.com/s3fs-public/publication/economic-impact-cybercrime.pdf.

Norton. 2017. "Cyber Security Insights Report Global Results." Norton (accessed April 11, 2023), https://now.symassets.com/content/dam/norton/global/pdfs/norton_cybersecurity_insights/NCSIR-global-results-US.pdf.

Piccotti, L. R., and H. Wang. 2022. "Informed Trading in the Options Market Surrounding Data Breaches." *Global Finance Journal* 56: 100774.

Świątkowska, J. 2020. "Tackling Cybercrime to Unleash Developing Countries' Digital Potential." Background Paper Series No. 33, Pathways for Prosperity Commission, Oxford, United Kingdom.

Tosun, O. K. 2021. "Cyber-Attacks and Stock Market Activity." *International Review of Financial Analysis* 76: 101795.

Vergara Cobos, E., and S. Cakir. Forthcoming. "A Review of the Economic Costs of Cyber Incidents." World Bank, Washington, DC.

Vergara Cobos, E., S. Cakir, H. Mei-Zahav, and B. Barakcin. Forthcoming. "The Role of Cybersecurity in Economic Performance." World Bank, Washington, DC.

Wang, B., P. Zheng, Y. Yin, A. Shih, and L. Wang. 2022. "Toward Human-Centric Smart Manufacturing: A Human-Cyber-Physical Systems (HCPS) Perspective." *Journal of Manufacturing Systems* 63: 471–90.

Wang, T., K. N. Kannan, and J. R. Ulmer. 2013. "The Association between the Disclosure and the Realization of Information Security Risk Factors." *Information Systems Research* 24 (2): 201–18.

CHAPTER 3

The Cybersecurity Market

Key Messages

Market growth

- Global spending on information security and risk management accounts for about 0.2 percent of the world's gross domestic product.

- This market is projected to surge by over 14 percent in 2024 compared to the previous year. Such a growth rate is nearly double that of projected information technology spending and nearly quadruple the projected growth of the global economy.

- Rapid growth is anticipated to continue in the market, particularly in the cloud security, data privacy, and data security sectors.

- However, spending on professional security services remains dominant, making up over 40 percent of the global market.

- Despite the growth, the cybersecurity industry is constrained by inadequate investment in research and development (R&D), low public cybersecurity awareness, and an estimated shortage of 4 million skilled cybersecurity professionals.

Demand characteristics

- North America accounts for over 50 percent of the global market, which is 16 times larger than the combined market size of Latin America and the Caribbean.

- Sales of cybersecurity products to small and medium enterprises (SMEs) have declined in recent years.

- SMEs and those at the lower end of the income distribution are less likely to be aware of cyber risks and more likely to be vulnerable to them.

- In Africa, about 90 percent of businesses lack cybersecurity measures, although 80 percent of large companies have established cybersecurity frameworks.

- The government's per capita budget for cybersecurity exceeds US$30 in Canada and the United States, but it is less than US$1 in highly targeted developing countries like India and Mexico.

Market failures

- Various factors affect the efficiency of the cybersecurity market, such as noninternalized systemic risk, insufficient investment in cybersecurity R&D, information asymmetry, vendor risk exposure, misaligned incentives, and unclear returns to investment.

- Low cybersecurity awareness among the general population creates downward pressure on both the prices and quality of resilient products.

- At least 90 percent of organizations worldwide maintain business ties with third-party vendors that have recently experienced a cyber incident. Yet, the majority does not mitigate third-party cyber risk.

- The information and communications and health care sectors face the highest vendor-related cyber risk, with averages of 25 and 15.5 third-party relationships, respectively.

- The financial sector has the lowest vendor cyber risk, managing an average of 6.5 third-party relationships.

- Cybersecurity investment is driven by a cost-saving rationale. However, unlike other cost-saving projects, the returns to cybersecurity investment are unquantifiable.

- Firms translate losses from cyber incidents into price hikes, which are assumed by consumers.

- Lack of transparency in the frequency and severity of cyber incidents and low public awareness affect market efficiency.

Government roles

- Governments in high-income countries largely influence market dynamics through substantial procurements, customized standards and certifications, and investments in R&D.

- Governments can boost market efficiency by investing in public cybersecurity awareness and training, and leading a strategic plan for cybersecurity R&D.

- Regulators can take an active role in protecting the energy, information and communications, and transport sectors, as well as other critical infrastructure closely connected to human rights protection.

Introduction

The cybersecurity industry is experiencing rapid growth and transformation, driven by various factors. These include the continuous increases of Internet of Things devices and the sophistication of cyberattacks, as well as more recent factors such as organizations' adoption of the cloud, the security challenges posed by modern artificial intelligence (AI), the replacement of virtual private networks with zero trust network access, the rise of hybrid work, and the evolving regulatory landscape.

Global security spending, as indicated by spending on information security and risk management, grew at twice the rate of the global economy in 2022, and it is projected to grow at over four times in 2024, representing spending of almost 0.2 percent of the world's gross domestic product (Gartner 2023a; IMF 2024). The 2024 expected growth rate of 14 percent will surpass the worldwide growth rate of information technology (IT) spending by at least 6 percentage points (Gartner 2024). Market growth is expected despite regional differences and a decrease in the small and medium enterprises (SMEs) submarket (WEF 2024).

Approximately 54 percent of global spending on cybersecurity comes from North America, which is 16 times larger than the combined spending of all the countries in Latin America and the Caribbean (Canalys 2022). North America holds the largest market share and hosts numerous specialized startups, centralizing the market in high-income countries (HICs). This centralization is driven by factors such as economic strength, a favorable regulatory environment, a concentration of technology companies, significant research and development (R&D) investment, an available skilled workforce, and access to capital.[1]

Demand growth is expected across all geographic regions, including in rapidly digitizing low- and middle-income countries, like India, where the cybersecurity market is projected to grow from US$3.97 billion in 2023 to US$9.2 billion by 2028, at a compound annual growth rate of 18.3 percent (Thakur 2024). The market is particularly expected to expand in newer and more security-challenging areas, such as cloud computing and data privacy (figure 3.1).

FIGURE 3.1 Global security and risk management end user spending for all segments, 2022–24

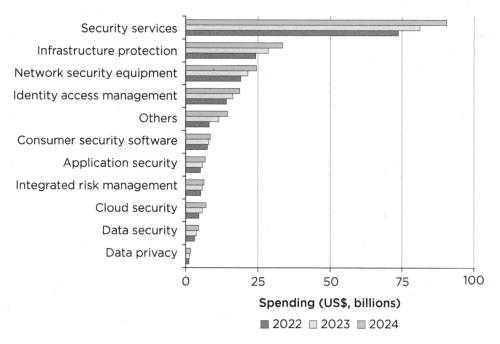

Spending (US$, billions)

■ 2022　□ 2023　■ 2024

Source: Original figure for this book, based on Gartner 2023a.

However, despite positive market trends, the cybersecurity industry faces two major constraints: insufficient investment in R&D and a shortage of skilled cybersecurity professionals. Investment in R&D is crucial to meet the growing demand and counter the increasing sophistication of cyberattacks. Yet, due to the rapidly evolving and unpredictable threat landscape, the benefits of cybersecurity R&D may not always be fully realized by the investors. This could result in an inadequate allocation of resources to this critical area.[2]

The cybersecurity industry is also significantly constrained by a shortage of skilled professionals needed to develop, implement, and manage cybersecurity solutions. Worldwide, there is a deficit of approximately 4 million cybersecurity professionals, and more than half of all companies report difficulties in filling information and communication technology (ICT) positions (European Commission 2022; ISC2 2023). This shortage makes it challenging to achieve an optimal level of societal cybersecurity. This could be particularly true in developing countries, like India, where the workforce gap increased by 40 percent in 2023 from 2022, and the largest economies in Sub-Saharan Africa, Nigeria and South Africa, where the gap increased by more than 10 percent. Moreover, with the largest workforce gaps seen in the health care sector, the security of the supply chain may emerge as one of the most significant risks to patient care (Kwolek 2024).

The cybersecurity workforce gap might not be the only labor problem, as global surveys suggest that over 90 percent of organizations worldwide could have cybersecurity skills gaps, which could be worse than the total worker shortage. In fact, 2023 showed an increasing number of layoffs despite the shortages of cybersecurity professionals (ISC2 2023). This phenomenon could explain the unmet demand for advanced cybersecurity skills influenced by the higher frequency and sophistication of cyberattacks.

Advancements in AI are expected to create new opportunities in the cybersecurity industry by facilitating security analyses, threat and vulnerability detection, and simplifying traditional security operation tools. Modern large language models can also enhance the field's appeal to talent by automating the most tedious and less desirable tasks, potentially helping to alleviate the workforce gap. However, AI-enabled cybersecurity automation also brings new challenges, such as expanding the cyberattack surface, raising ethical and legal concerns, and increasing the speed and scale of cyberattacks (for example, through the development of advanced automated attack tools). This challenging reality underscores the growing need for investment in R&D to ensure the efficient and ethical development of AI-enabled cybersecurity solutions.

This chapter explores the current state of the cybersecurity market, highlighting key characteristics, such as the emerging cybersecurity gap among users, the strong market impact of governments in HICs, and possible sources of market failures. It concludes with a discussion on the crucial roles of governments, which include protecting critical infrastructure, raising public cybersecurity awareness and training, and strategic planning for R&D.

The New Digital Gap: The Cybersecurity Gap

The demand for cybersecurity comes from various scales of applications. Small-scale applications used by individuals and small businesses are mainly driven by the need to protect sensitive data, ensure the operability of devices, secure remote work, and mitigate financial risks. Medium-scale applications in businesses and organizations mainly focus on protecting customer and employee data, intellectual property, mitigation of financial and reputational risks, regulatory compliance, and operational continuity. Large-scale cybersecurity applications refer to comprehensive and advanced measures to protect large-scale firms, critical infrastructures, and governmental or international organizations. These applications are designed to address the complex security needs of such entities. Many of these applications are inherently private. However, building resiliency in cyberspace is at the center of discussions of public investment.

Despite the booming cybersecurity market, a significant divide is emerging between individuals and organizations. The cybersecurity gap could become the new digital gap as those in the lower end of the income distribution are less likely to be aware of cyber risks and to invest in cybersecurity, thereby facing higher exposure to cyber incidents (Sultan 2019).[3]

For low-income individuals, this could imply higher exposure to online identity theft.[4] Online identity theft is the top cybercrime activity targeting individuals and the top cybersecurity concern for the average internet user (Gallup 2021) (figure 3.2). Since the COVID-19 pandemic, there has been an increase in online identity theft (mainly from phishing emails and business email compromise), facilitated by the development of cybercrime as a service and cryptocurrencies.[5] This has led to high levels of concern across several regions. Among internet users, 62 percent in Central and Western Africa, 61 percent in Southeast Asia, 60 percent in Southern Africa, 56 percent in Latin America and the Caribbean, and 54 percent in Eastern Africa claimed to be "very worried" about online identity theft (Gallup 2021). Other top online threats to individuals across the globe include nonpayment or nondelivery, personal data breaches, and extortion (FBI 2021).

FIGURE 3.2 **The market for stolen credentials**

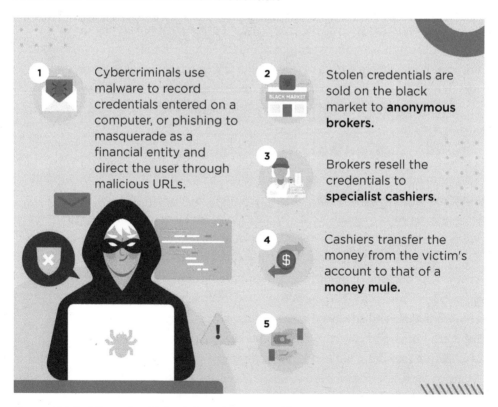

1 Cybercriminals use malware to record credentials entered on a computer, or phishing to masquerade as a financial entity and direct the user through malicious URLs.

2 Stolen credentials are sold on the black market to **anonymous brokers.**

3 Brokers resell the credentials to **specialist cashiers.**

4 Cashiers transfer the money from the victim's account to that of a **money mule.**

5

Source: Original figure for this book, based on Moore 2010.

At the business level, cybersecurity investments are mainly prioritized by the largest and most profitable organizations, with the primary reason for investing being regulations solely directed at large companies (Westlands Advisory 2023). SMEs, which account for 90 percent of the world's businesses, continue to struggle to prioritize cybersecurity, presenting important cybersecurity gaps and stagnant annual security budgets or headcounts (Chidukwani, Zander, Koutsakis 2022; DigitalOcean 2023). Among the SMEs that have implemented cybersecurity measures, the most common tools include two-factor authentication (59 percent of SMEs), virus or malware protection (41 percent), and employee training on phishing scams.[6] The levels of cybersecurity among businesses can also be observed in developing regions like Africa, where approximately 90 percent of businesses have not put any cybersecurity measure in place, while over 60 percent of large companies have adopted data protection and governance approaches, and 80 percent have established cybersecurity frameworks (KPMG 2022). Moreover, with the rising salaries and recruitment costs of cybersecurity professionals, the financial burden and cyber risk of smaller organizations are increasing, especially for those that operate businesses processing large amounts of personal and sensitive data (Misheva 2023).

In the cyber insurance market, small organizations are three times less likely to be cyber insured than large organizations by revenue and four times less likely than large organizations by number of employees (WEF 2024).[7] Following a data breach, cyber insurance is the least prioritized measure. After a data breach, most targeted organizations focus on response planning and testing (50 percent), employee training (46 percent), and threat detection and response technologies (38 percent), while only 18 percent invest in cyber insurance (IBM 2023).

The Market Influence of Governments in HICs

Governments in HICs significantly influence global market dynamics by procuring cybersecurity technologies and capabilities, typically on a large scale. The global cybersecurity market is projected to grow at an 11 percent compound annual growth rate from 2020 to 2027, with spending from the government sector accounting for about 36 percent of the market, primarily driven by demand from the United States.[8] In contrast, developing countries have much smaller cybersecurity budgets and less market influence. For example, the per capita government budget for cybersecurity exceeds US$30 in Canada and the United States, but it is about US$1 in highly targeted developing countries like Mexico and India.[9]

The demand for cybersecurity professionals is also large across government sectors. For example, in the United States, government demand for cybersecurity professionals grew by 58 percent from 2019 to 2023, while private sector demand grew by 36 percent (Lightcast Press Office 2023). However, given the worldwide shortage of cybersecurity professionals and the increasing salaries and hiring costs, governments worldwide, especially in developing countries, are struggling to compete with the private sector. Such is the case that in 2023, there were cybersecurity staffing shortages in 78 percent of the nonmilitary government sectors worldwide (ISC2 2023).

Governments in HICs have even larger market power through the enforcement of standards, certifications, and regulations, as well as fines and other compliance mechanisms. Many HICs have an agency responsible for developing cybersecurity standards and certification systems for their national government's use or the use of industries within their borders, creating different market incentives and skill thresholds worldwide (Rains 2023). For example, Germany is the single largest market in the European Union, making the standards published by the German Federal Office of Information Security highly influential in European markets. Standards aim to improve security by defining the functional and assurance requirements that information products and systems must have, enabling consistency among developers, and serving as a reliability metric. Cybersecurity certifications could serve as one of the most powerful instruments for addressing cybersecurity concerns before market deployment (Matheu et al. 2020).[10] This can be done by creating demand incentives among private and public operators to prioritize cybersecurity over price when procuring goods and services, especially for high-risk or strategic assets. At the same time, the publication of standards and certifications can change suppliers' behaviors through an interest in doing business with domestic and foreign governments and proving the quality of their products.

Cybersecurity Market Failures

Market failure occurs when the allocation of goods and services facilitated by the market is Pareto inefficient, which implies that it is possible to improve social welfare without making anyone worse off. Pareto inefficiency can occur because certain goods are not traded or because the market on its own reaches an equilibrium that is not competitive (Hammond 1998). In cybersecurity, it is widely acknowledged that the resilience of one digital asset is contingent on the resilience of others, and the overall resilience of cyberspace depends on the security of its most vulnerable components (figure 3.3). Hence, in principle, an efficient cybersecurity market allocation would maximize the smooth operation of systems in cyberspace, with no alternative allocation improving overall resilience without being detrimental to anyone.

Market failures are usually the justification for nonmarket alternatives like government interventions, under the argument that policy makers can and should make participants better off (Ledyard 1989). However, the need for regulation hinges on demonstrating policy makers' unique capacity to address sources of market failures and attain a more efficient allocation without causing adverse market or societal effects.

FIGURE 3.3 **Cybersecurity prisoner's dilemma**

		Company B	
		Secure	**Insecure**
Company A	**Secure**	Both gain an incentive of 40.	Company A gets an incentive of 25, while Company B gets an incentive of 50.
	Insecure	Company A gets an incentive of 50, while Company B gets an incentive of 25.	Both gain an incentive of 30.

Source: Kelly 2017.
Note: Kelly (2017) demonstrates the interdependency in cyberspace and its externalities through this prisoner's dilemma example, which represents the incentives of two companies, A and B, to invest in securing their information technology assets to prevent their networks from being used to attack other companies.

Underinvestment in R&D

Given the wide range of cyber threats and vulnerabilities, along with the rapidly evolving sophistication of cyberattacks, organizations investing in cybersecurity R&D may not fully realize the potential gains. This could lead to an insufficient allocation of resources to this crucial area. Without proper economic incentives and a strategic plan for cybersecurity priorities, the market might fail to develop innovative and efficient solutions, leaving systems vulnerable to newer and more sophisticated cyber threats.

Investment in cybersecurity R&D is vital for enhancing cybersecurity capabilities and tackling the growing complexity and severity of cyberattacks. As new attack methods emerge and the cyberattack surface expands, R&D plays a key role in developing advanced solutions to replace rapidly outdated technologies. Moreover, while attackers need only exploit a single vulnerability to breach a system, defenders must safeguard against numerous potential weaknesses. Therefore, R&D is also essential for creating efficient and innovative security measures, such as improving threat detection speed and accuracy, predictive models, incident response, among others.

Despite its importance, cybersecurity R&D faces several challenges, including limited funding, a shortage of skilled cybersecurity professionals, high technological development costs, rapidly evolving threats, insufficient data on cybersecurity measures, a centralized industry in HICs, and a lack of coordination among organizations, academia, and governments. Overcoming these obstacles requires a coordinated effort from all stakeholders and increased funding opportunities (The White House 2023a) (figure 3.4). Additionally, it necessitates a strategic approach to cybersecurity funding and initiatives. Such a strategy should identify critical cybersecurity areas, address outdated technologies and practices, identify critical infrastructure, and target market failures (Benzel 2015).

FIGURE 3.4 Critical cybersecurity dependencies and priorities in the United States

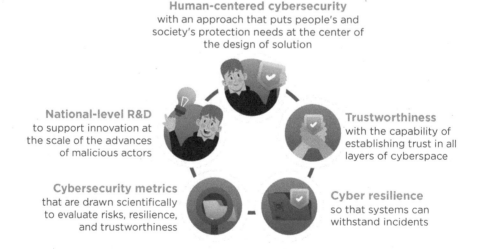

Human-centered cybersecurity with an approach that puts people's and society's protection needs at the center of the design of solution

National-level R&D to support innovation at the scale of the advances of malicious actors

Cybersecurity metrics that are drawn scientifically to evaluate risks, resilience, and trustworthiness

Trustworthiness with the capability of establishing trust in all layers of cyberspace

Cyber resilience so that systems can withstand incidents

Source: Original figure for this book based on The White House 2023a.
Note: R&D = research and development.

Information asymmetries

Different factors affect asymmetric information in cybersecurity markets, including the credence good (or professional good) nature of the cybersecurity and digital product markets, and the potential damage to reputation and customer relationships that heightens reticence in information sharing. The former results in unreliable information spread in the community, which is evident in the lack of accurate and reliable data on cyber incidents and incurred costs, which can lead to misinformed market participants and inefficient levels of investment in cybersecurity (Kopp, Kaffenberger, and Wilson 2017; Moore 2010). In this sense, cyber personas cannot fully assess the level of cyber risk they face, lack enough information to make informed decisions about how to manage it, but also cannot assess the effectiveness of their purchased cybersecurity measures prior to a cyberattack.

Regulated standards or mandates to disclose cyber incidents could alleviate asymmetric information. Moreover, research shows that there is an average decrease in shareholder risk, proxied by the cost of equity, after the implementation of disclosure laws. Such laws also appear to have a positive effect on cybersecurity investments and the demand for cybersecurity expertise among firms (Ashraf and Sunder 2023). Among the prominent examples, the European Union's General Data Protection Regulation (GDPR) establishes a strict set of rules for personal data permissions. These include requiring breached companies to notify all affected people and the authority within 72 hours of the breach. Failure to comply with the GDPR could result in a fine of up to €20 million or 4 percent of the annual global revenue, whichever is larger. Similarly, the 2017 Chinese law requires that any cyber incident compromising more than 100,000 users leads to an investigation and evaluation process reported to the government within five days. India, where the government is the most targeted sector in disclosed cyber incidents, mandates one of the strictest reporting rules in the world, with a six-hour reporting window in the event of a major cyber incident.[11,12]

Mitigating asymmetric information through regulation has also been done in the area of ransomware protection. For example, after the Colonial Pipeline ransomware attack that shut down a major US pipeline system in 2021, the federal government issued an Executive Order on Improving the Nation's Cybersecurity, which aimed, among other things, to remove barriers to threat information sharing between the government and the private sector.

However, policy makers must also consider that disclosing cyber incidents negatively impacts organizations' economic performance and reputation (see chapter 2). The question of how legislation will affect cybersecurity market failures and the overall economy will only grow in importance as a more regulated future is expected. Estimations show that by 2025, 30 percent of nations will pass new cybersecurity legislation in the domain of ransomware payments, fines, negotiations, and other newer challenges (Gartner 2023b). Key aspects of the successful creation of positive cybersecurity impacts will depend on the legislation's ability to deal with the cross-jurisdiction presence of malicious actors, anonymity, reputational damage from disclosure, and the evolving nature of cybercrime (Khan et al. 2022; Rains 2023).

At a more granular level, asymmetric information is also present in the market for digital products. Cybersecurity components for digital products could be facing downward pressure on both prices and quality due to consumers' limited cybersecurity awareness and knowledge about the vulnerabilities of the products. As in a credence good market, consumers often lack the expertise to determine the cybersecurity features that are needed for their digital products to operate appropriately, forcing them to rely on sellers' "diagnosis and treatment." Sellers' expertise not only provides them opportunities to defraud consumers (Liu, Vergara-Cobos, and Zhou 2019), but also creates a phenomenon referred to by the theory as the "market for lemons." With research showing that the general population lags in knowledge of the existing cybersecurity tools and overall cybersecurity (Zwilling et al. 2022), consumers' lack of cybersecurity awareness could result in the market price being set at a level such that only the "bad lemons," or digital devices with weak cybersecurity capacities, are offered.

Reduced incentives for risk mitigation

Asymmetric information leads to moral hazard, or a situation in which one party is more likely to take risks because they do not bear the full consequences of those risks. When a cyber incident occurs, the negative consequences (such as financial losses, data breaches, and reputational damage) are often shared between the company and its stakeholders. For instance, a cyber incident could lead to customers becoming more vulnerable to identity theft, financial losses, and even price hikes, while shareholders might see a decline in stock value. Because the burden is shared, companies may adopt a more relaxed approach to risk mitigation, knowing that they are not fully accountable for the losses. According to a survey by IBM (2023) across 16 countries and 17 industries, 57 percent of compromised firms reported that data breaches led to an increase in the prices for their goods and services.

Moral hazard is particularly present in the absence of liability regulations. For example, in the case of the adoption of cyber insurance in unregulated insurance markets, research shows that the insured agents decrease their cybersecurity commitments, leading to a more insecure network (Khalili, Naghizadeh, and Liu 2017; Moore and Anderson 2011).

Investment in cybersecurity awareness is pivotal for correcting for asymmetric information and moral hazard. However, translating awareness efforts into practical defenses and positive market effects remains a challenge (ITU 2013; Shafqat and Masood 2016; Zwilling et al. 2022). There is a variety of considerations for designing awareness plans, such as understandability, inclusivity, constancy, and customization based on the cultural context and audience characteristics (Bada, Sasse, and Nurse 2019; Chang and Coppel 2020; De Bruijn and Janssen 2017). Other instruments, such as cybersecurity labels and software bills of materials, are promising tools for empowering consumers to make more-informed decisions and guiding them toward more security-focused decisions (Caven and Camp 2023). However, the effectiveness of these instruments will depend on the costs of testing and upgrading, usability, acceptability, and understandability.

Vendor risk exposure

The supply chain of modern companies often relies on third-party vendors and the sharing of information across networks. This situation expands organizations' cyberattack surface, with research showing that the largest portion of third-party incidents are related to cyber risk, and the majority of organizations may have experienced a data breach caused by one of their third parties.[13] Yet, organizations do not usually monitor the security and privacy practices of their vendors or have a comprehensive inventory of all the third parties with whom they share sensitive information (Ponemon Institute 2022).

Numerous organizations remain unaware of the inherent vulnerabilities associated with third-party relationships and often focus solely on their internal risk. Indeed, data from more than 200,000 organizations in the Americas, Asia, and Europe show that more than 90 percent of organizations maintain business ties with at least one vendor that has had a cybersecurity breach. Notably, the information and communications sector leads in the number of third-party relationships, with an average of 25 third-party connections, followed by health care with 15.5, while the financial sector has the lowest, at 6.5. Organizations that lack robust security protocols tend to involve themselves with double the number of third-party vendors and tenfold the number of fourth-party entities. Moreover, for each third-party vendor, organizations generally have indirect relationships with 60 to 90 times as many fourth parties (SecurityScorecard and Cyentia 2024).

Internalization of systemic risk

Cyber risk is a textbook example of a systemic risk (Kopp, Kaffenberger, and Wilson 2017). The debate over cybersecurity regulation revolves around the concept of externalities and the extent to which market participants internalize cyber risks that can lead to systemic failures. Although highly concerning cases of systemic failures, such as cyber runs, have not occurred yet, the number of cases in which cyber incidents have translated into second- and even third-run effects is vast (see chapter 2). Systemic risk is a negative externality that is particularly present in highly technological and financially interconnected sectors. Failure to address systemic negative externalities can lead to inadequate investment levels by private organizations compared to what is socially ideal. With limited organizational budgets and the centralization of the cybersecurity market in HICs, internalization of systemic risk might be more challenging across organizations in developing countries (Hiller, Kisska-Schulze, and Shackelford 2024).

Data privacy regulations worldwide have pushed firms to internalize some of the cyber risks faced by their consumers and stakeholders. Such regulations are becoming increasingly popular; however, according to the UN Trade and Development organization, 15 percent of countries worldwide do not yet have data protection and privacy legislation, and 9 percent only have a draft legislation. All these lagging nations are developing countries, and most are in Africa.

Taxation of compromised firms has been one of the proposed solutions for fostering internalization of cyber risk. For example, in the European Union, the GDPR allows for significant fines for data breaches and violations of data protection laws. Although it is not explicitly a tax, the revenue generated from these fines could be considered a form of financial penalty akin to taxation.

Misaligned incentives in the markets for digital products

Creating robust digital products and services is a significant challenge because misaligned incentives often push producers to compromise on product resilience in favor of short-term gains (Huang, Biczók, and Liu 2024). The question of *how to build robust digital systems and products efficiently* is an ongoing task for producers, researchers, and the overall cybersecurity community (Sarker 2023).

As with R&D, attempts to create robust digital systems and products usually require large amounts of resources. However, given the rapid technological innovation, the technological market's tendencies to reward first movers, the high competition, and the short product life cycles, producers of digital products have incentives to prioritize fast release over security testing.

Moreover, instead of opting for standard processes and sources that have undergone analysis and testing, producers frequently choose proprietary and less transparent production alternatives to lock in customers, increase switching costs, and increase the investment required by competitors to develop compatible products.

Unclear returns on investment

Finally, there is a strong incentive among firms to underinvest in cybersecurity, driven by a lack of clarity on the returns on investment (Gordon, Loeb, and Lucyshyn 2014). Investments in IT typically aim to create value, but investments in cybersecurity aim to minimize losses. However, uncertainty about the cost of cyber incidents and the probability of occurrence complicates understanding of the cost-saving rationale for cybersecurity investments. Although exploited vulnerabilities can result in significant losses for the targeted organizations and the network, there is considerable uncertainty about whether such costs will materialize or if they will be high enough to justify investing in product robustness and overall cybersecurity (Huang, Biczók, and Liu 2024).

How many vulnerabilities need to be exploited to hack a system? Usually, one is enough. Thus, producers can spend millions trying to make their products more robust, yet malicious actors may need to spend only a small amount of resources to breach a system. Given the uncertainty behind the returns to cybersecurity investments, producers have adopted alternative suboptimal strategies, such as timed or delayed investments. This alternative proposes investing a portion of the cybersecurity budget and deferring the rest until a cyber incident occurs (Chronopoulos, Panaousis, and Grossklags 2017; Gordon, Loeb, and Lucyshyn 2003).

Critical Cybersecurity

Critical infrastructures are assets, whether physical or virtual, that are fundamental to the minimum functioning of a society and its economy.

The prolonged disruption of critical infrastructures reduces the flow of essential goods and services, creating a debilitating impact on national security, public health, and overall social welfare.[14] Although not all elements of critical infrastructure are critical, cybersecurity is essential as most critical infrastructure relies on a spectrum of software-based control systems for smooth, reliable, and continuous operation (Brunner and Suter 2008; Moteff et al. 2003; Weber, Pericàs Riera, and Laumann 2023).

Cybersecurity in the critical infrastructure context is filled with positive externalities (Kelly 2017), spanning the provision of utilities, such as energy and water, as well as transport, finance, telecommunications, health care, and education. Various types of critical infrastructure are linked in a complex IT architecture, and many are operated by multiple providers, including private sector entities. Therefore, the provision of essential services can constitute a complex network, with real challenges in assessing and identifying the cyber risks.

Critical infrastructure protection requires government-led, comprehensive efforts that join all stakeholders, including critical infrastructure owners and operators (World Bank 2023). For example, the US National Cybersecurity Strategy highlights the need for all stakeholders, sectoral regulators, critical infrastructure owners and operators, product vendors, and service providers to collaborate effectively to build innovative capabilities to confront and manage cyber risks to critical infrastructure (The White House 2023b). This could tackle the liability challenges that remain in most critical infrastructure protection programs.

Although many HICs have identified sets of critical infrastructures (in the United States, 16 sectors; Japan, 13 sectors; Singapore, 11 sectors; and Germany, 8 sectors),[15] less than half of developing countries have defined critical infrastructure sectors. Lack of identification is present mainly in Africa, Asia, Latin America and the Caribbean, and Oceania (figure 3.5). Nonetheless, recent research shows the most frequently considered critical infrastructure sector is energy (96 percent of the surveyed countries), followed by ICT (95 percent), transport (93 percent), economy and finance (89 percent), public services (84 percent), and health (83 percent), with energy, ICT, and transport being well-established within the human rights framework under international or national laws (Weber, Pericàs Riera, and Laumann 2023).

FIGURE 3.5 Share of countries that have defined critical infrastructure sectors, 2023

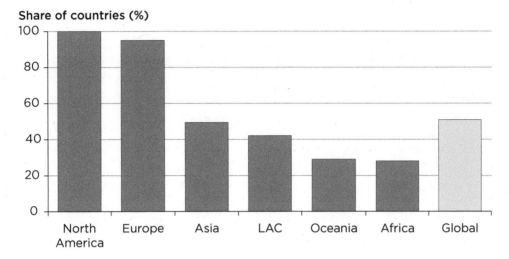

Share of countries (%)

Source: Original figure for this book, based on Weber, Pericàs Riera, and Laumann 2023.
Note: North America only includes Canada and the United States. LAC = Latin America and the Caribbean.

Policy Recommendations

- *Planning and investment in R&D.* Governments must incentivize R&D investment in cybersecurity to address emerging threats. This could involve incentives such as grants, or public-private partnerships to stimulate innovation in the national industry. Moreover, governments must lead a national cybersecurity R&D plan to unify efforts in the most critical areas.

- *Public awareness campaigns.* Policies could help to increase demand for cybersecurity products and services, boost the national industry, and minimize sources of market failures.

- *Support for cybersecurity education and training.* Governments and private sector stakeholders can collaborate to address the shortage of skilled cybersecurity professionals. Initiatives such as scholarships, apprenticeships, and vocational training programs can help to cultivate a skilled workforce to meet the labor demand. These efforts must address the continuous need for advanced skills.

- *Collaboration on risk management efforts for critical infrastructure protection.* These efforts are especially crucial for infrastructure that provides essential services, like energy, water, transport, and communications.

- *Support for SMEs.* Policies could be implemented to assist SMEs in enhancing their cybersecurity posture. This could include providing access to affordable cybersecurity tools, training, and resources tailored to the needs and limitations of smaller organizations.

- *Regulatory frameworks for data protection and privacy.* Governments should enact and enforce robust and up-to-date regulations to protect individuals' data privacy and ensure secure handling of sensitive information, helping to mitigate cyber risks and build trust in digital platforms.

- *International collaboration and information sharing.* Governments should foster collaboration and information sharing among stakeholders at the national and international levels to address cyber threats effectively, especially those related to critical infrastructure, such as energy, communications, water, and transport.

- *Incentives for adopting best practices.* Governments can encourage organizations (especially vendors) to adopt best practices in cybersecurity through regulatory incentives or certification programs, as well as procurement preferences for those that meet the standards.

- *Promotion of public-private partnerships.* Governments could facilitate public-private partnerships to leverage the expertise and resources of both sectors in addressing cybersecurity challenges. Collaborative initiatives can enhance cyber resilience and response capabilities across industries.

- *Focus on emerging technologies.* Policy makers should pay particular attention to the cybersecurity implications of emerging technologies, such as modern AI and cloud computing. Regulations and standards should be updated to address new risks and ensure the security of these technologies.

- *Market support.* Policies could support cybersecurity startups, especially those in highly interconnected and critical sectors.

Notes

1. Companies such as Palo Alto Networks, Cisco Systems, Fortinet, Check Point Software Technologies, and Crowd Strike rank as the market leaders with almost 30 percent of the global market in terms of total sales (Canalys 2022). These market leaders show staggering end-of-year market cap growth, especially since the COVID-19 pandemic. The industry also features a significant number of specialized startups and other emerging players (for example, firms focusing on niche areas, such as threat intelligence, endpoint protection, and identity management) introducing innovative cybersecurity technologies, although they are largely centered in HICs.

2. Additionally, R&D is resource intensive and is often financed through volatile funding sources, making it more susceptible to adverse economic shocks, including cyber incidents. Evidence indicates that an increase in cyber incidents correlates with a long-term decline of at least 10 percent in overall R&D spending among firms in the year following the incident (He, Frost, and Pinsker 2020). The negative impact of cyber risk on R&D investment is primarily observed in high-tech and complex industries (Lattanzio and Ma 2023).

3. Human errors or misuse play a role in 74 percent of data breaches worldwide, and nearly 59 percent of internet users have not read a single privacy policy (Bada, von Solms, and Agrafiotis 2019).

4. This refers to fraudulently obtaining personal information from a victim for economic gain, for example, through credit card fraud and government documents or benefits fraud, and acquiring personal data and passwords to take over people's online accounts (Gallup 2021).

5. Microsoft (2021). Business email compromise is the costliest financial cybercrime, with an estimated US$2.4 billion in adjusted losses in 2021, representing more than 59 percent of the top five types of internet crime losses globally (FBI 2021). Moreover, according to Microsoft (2021), there are more than 83 million unique cryptocurrency wallets, a number that grew by 270 percent from 2017 to 2021, while spending on blockchain solutions grew by 340 percent in the same period.

6. These statistics are based on a survey conducted by DigitalOcean in 2023. The survey included responses from 554 founders, chief executive officers, and senior executives and managers and vice president–level executives at startups and small businesses in 76 countries (27 percent in the United States, 8 percent in the United Kingdom, and 5 percent in India) (DigitalOcean 2023).

7. Only 21 percent of organizations with fewer than 250 employees and 25 percent of organizations with profits of less than US$250 million have cyber insurance, while 85 percent of those with more than 100,000 employees and 75 percent of organizations with yearly profits greater than US$5.5 billion are cyber insured (WEF 2024).

8. By 2027, the global government cybersecurity market is expected to be valued at US$78.6 billion (Verified Market Reports 2023; https://www.linkedin.com/pulse /cybersecurity-market-latest-analysis-growth-forecast-2027-eric-martin/).

9. The sources for countries' government budgets and spending are (1) United States: the 2022 budget (https://www.whitehouse.gov/wp-content/uploads/2022/03/ap_16_it_fy2023.pdf); (2) Canada: the budget is US$875 million over five years, with US$238 million ongoing (https://www.budget.canada.ca/2023/pdf/budget-2023-en.pdf); (3) Mexico: the budget for cybersecurity in 2023 (https://mexicobusiness.news/tech/news/look-progress-proposed -federal-cybersecurity-law); and (4) India: more than US$48 million for cybersecurity projects in 2023–24 (https://www.indiabudget.gov.in/doc/eb/sbe27.pdf).

10. According to Rains (2023), US organizations mainly follow the National Institute of Standards and Technology (NIST) standards, mainly NIST SP 800-53 and NIST SP 800-171, while organizations in other parts of the world mostly follow the standards from the International Organization for Standardization or those from government standards

bodies, such as Germany's Federal Office of Information Security. There are also nongovernmental organizations that develop cybersecurity standards, such as the Internet Engineering Task Force.

11. See Dataminr (2023), https://www.dataminr.com/resources/insight/4-regions-with-new -and-changing-cybersecurity-legislation/.

12. According to the US Department of Justice, "a cyber incident should be reported if it:
    - May impact national security, economic security, or public health and safety,
    - Affects core government or critical infrastructure functions,
    - Results in a significant loss of data, system availability, or control of systems,
    - Involves a large number of victims,
    - Indicates unauthorized access to, or malicious software present on, critical information technology systems,
    - Violates federal law." (https://www.justice.gov/usao-ct/page/file/906222/dl).

13. The largest portion of third-party incidents in 2020 were related to cyber risk, with 17 percent of organizations claiming to have faced a high-impact, third-party risk incident affecting customer services, financial results, and reputation. Yet, over half of the surveyed organizations estimate that they are not investing enough in extended risk management (Deloitte Global 2020). According to Ponemon Institute (2022), nearly 60 percent of organizations in North America and Western Europe with a third-party risk management program may have experienced a data breach caused by one of their third parties.

14. Lewis (2006). Critical infrastructure integrates complex physical and cyber systems that are vulnerable to cyber threats, and their incapacity or destruction has debilitating effects on national security, economic stability, and public health and safety (National Institute of Standards and Technology definition of critical infrastructure).

15. Countries like the United States have identified a long list of critical industries, including food and water systems, agriculture, health systems and emergency services, IT and telecommunications, banking and finance, energy (electrical, nuclear, gas and oil, and dams), transportation (air, road, and port waterways), chemical and defense industries, postal and shipping entities, and national monuments and icons.

References

Ashraf, M., and J. Sunder. 2023. "Can Shareholders Benefit from Consumer Protection Disclosure Mandates? Evidence from Data Breach Disclosure Laws." *Accounting Review* 98 (4): 1–32.

Bada, M., A. M. Sasse, and J. R. Nurse. 2019. "Cyber Security Awareness Campaigns: Why Do They Fail to Change Behaviour?" arXiv preprint arXiv: 1901.02672.

Bada, M., B. von Solms, and I. Agrafiotis. 2019. "Reviewing National Cybersecurity Awareness in Africa: An Empirical Study." *International Journal on Advances in Security* 12 (1 & 2). http://www.iariajournals.org/security/.

Benzel, T. 2015. "A Strategic Plan for Cybersecurity Research and Development." *IEEE Security & Privacy* 13 (4): 3–5.

Brunner, E. M., and M. Suter. 2008. *International CIIP Handbook 2008/2009: An Inventory of 25 National and 7 International Critical Information Infrastructure Protection Policies.* ETH Zürich, Switzerland: Center for Security Studies.

Canalys. 2022. "Cybersecurity Market Grows 16% Despite Deteriorating Economic Conditions." Canalys, Singapore. https://canalys-prod-public.s3.eu-west-1.amazonaws.com /static/press_release/2022/1041161511Canalys-Cybsersecruity-market-review-Q3-2022.pdf.

Caven, P., and L. J. Camp. 2023. "Towards a More Secure Ecosystem: Implications for Cybersecurity Labels and SBOMs." Available at SSRN 4527526.

Chang, L. Y., and N. Coppel. 2020. "Building Cyber Security Awareness in a Developing Country: Lessons from Myanmar." *Computers & Security* 97: 101959.

Chidukwani, A., S. Zander, and P. Koutsakis. 2022. "A Survey on the Cyber Security of Small-to-Medium Businesses: Challenges, Research Focus and Recommendations." *IEEE Access* 10: 85701–19.

Chronopoulos, M., E. Panaousis, and J. Grossklags. 2017. "An Options Approach to Cybersecurity Investment." *IEEE Access* 6: 12175–86.

Dataminr. 2023. "4 Regions with New and Changing Cybersecurity Legislation." Dataminr, New York. https://www.dataminr.com/resources/insight/4-regions-with-new-and-changing -cybersecurity-legislation/.

De Bruijn, H., and M. Janssen. 2017. "Building Cybersecurity Awareness: The Need for Evidence-Based Framing Strategies." *Government Information Quarterly* 34 (1): 1–7.

Deloitte Global. 2020. "Extended Enterprise Risk Management Survey." Deloitte Global, London. https://www.deloitte.com/global/en/about/press-room/third-party-failures-can -cost-companies-as-much-as-us-1-billion-per-incident-per-a-recent-deloitte-survey.html.

DigitalOcean. 2023. "Currents." DigitalOcean, New York. https://www.digitalocean.com /currents/may-2023#currents-form.

European Commission. 2022. "Digital Economy and Society Index (DESI) 2022." European Commission, Brussels, Belgium.

FBI (Federal Bureau of Investigation). 2021. "Internet Crime Report 2021." FBI, Washington, DC. https://www.ic3.gov/Media/PDF/AnnualReport/2021_IC3Report.pdf.

Gallup. 2021. "World Risk Poll 2021: A Changed World?" Gallup, Washington, DC.

Gartner. 2023a. "Gartner Forecasts Global Security and Risk Management Spending to Grow 14% in 2024." Gartner, San Francisco, CA (accessed April 8, 2024), https://www.gartner.com /en/newsroom/press-releases/2023-09-28-gartner-forecasts-global-security-and-risk -management-spending-to-grow-14-percent-in-2024.

Gartner. 2023b. "Gartner Security & Risk Management Summit 2023 India: Day 1 Highlights." Gartner, San Francisco, CA. https://www.gartner.com/en/newsroom/press-releases /2023-02-13-gartner-security-risk-management-summit-mumbai-day1-highlights#:~:text =Through%202025%2C%2030%25%20of%20nation,as%20well%20as%20encrypt%20it.

Gartner. 2024. "Planning for GenAI Initiatives Is Helping to Drive IT Spending in 2024 and Beyond." Gartner, San Francisco, CA (accessed July 21, 2024), https://www.gartner.com/en /newsroom/press-releases/2024-04-16-gartner-forecast-worldwide-it-spending-to-grow-8

-percent-in-2024#:~:text=Worldwide%20IT%20spending%20is%20expected,the%20
end%20of%20the%20decade.

Gordon, L. A., M. P. Loeb, and W. Lucyshyn. 2003. "Sharing Information on Computer Systems Security: An Economic Analysis." *Journal of Accounting and Public Policy* 22 (6): 461–85.

Gordon, L. A., M. P. Loeb, and W. Lucyshyn. 2014. "Cybersecurity Investments in the Private Sector: The Role of Governments." *Georgetown Journal of International Affairs* 15: 79–88.

Hammond, P. 1998. "The Efficiency Theorems and Market Failure." In *Elements of General Equilibrium Analysis*, edited by A. P. Kirman, 211–60. Oxford, UK: Blackwell Publishers.

He, C. Z., T. Frost, and R. E. Pinsker. 2020. "The Impact of Reported Cybersecurity Breaches on Firm Innovation." *Journal of Information Systems* 34 (2): 187–209.

Hiller, J., K. Kisska-Schulze, and S. Shackelford. 2024. "Cybersecurity Carrots and Sticks." *American Business Law Journal* 61 (1): 5–29.

Huang, Z., G. Biczók, and M. Liu. 2024. "Incentivizing Secure Software Development: The Role of Liability (Waiver) and Audit." arXiv preprint arXiv: 2401.08476.

IBM. 2023. "2023 Cost of a Data Breach." IBM, Armonk, NY.

IMF (International Monetary Fund). 2024. *World Economic Outlook: The Global Economy in a Sticky Spot*. Washington, DC: IMF.

ISC2 (International Information System Security Certification Consortium). 2023. "How the Economy, Skills Gap and Artificial Intelligence Are Challenging the Global Cybersecurity Workforce." ISC2, Alexandria, VA.

ITU (International Telecommunication Union). 2013. "ITU Survey on Measures Taken to Raise Awareness on Cybersecurity." ITU, Geneva.

Kelly, D. 2017. "The Economics of Cybersecurity." In *Proceedings of the 12th International Conference on Cyber Warfare and Security*, edited by A. R. Bryant, J. R. Lopez, and R. F. Mills, 522. Academic Conferences International Limited.

Khalili, M. M., P. Naghizadeh, and M. Liu. 2017. "Designing Cyber Insurance Policies: Mitigating Moral Hazard through Security Pre-screening." In *Game Theory for Networks: 7th International EAI Conference Proceedings*, 63–73. Springer International.

Khan, S., T. Saleh, M. Dorasamy, N. Khan, O. Tan Swee Leng, and R. Gale Vergara. 2022. "A Systematic Literature Review on Cybercrime Legislation." *F1000Research* 11: 971.

Kopp, E., L. Kaffenberger, and C. Wilson. 2017. "Cyber Risk, Market Failures, and Financial Stability." Working Paper No. 2017/185, International Monetary Fund, Washington, DC.

KPMG. 2022. "KPMG's Africa Cyber Security Outlook 2022 Survey." KPMG, Amstelveen, Netherlands. https://kpmg.com/ke/en/home/insights/2022/09/Africa%20Cyber%20Outlook%20launch.html.

Kwolek, B. 2024. "A Cybersecurity Odyssey: Between Scylla and Charybdis." *Healthcare Management Forum* 37 (1): 5–8.

Lattanzio, G., and Y. Ma. 2023. "Cybersecurity Risk and Corporate Innovation." *Journal of Corporate Finance* 82: 102445.

Ledyard, J. O. 1989. "Market Failure." In *Allocation, Information and Markets*, edited by M. Milgate, P. K. Newman, J. Eatwell, and B. Eatwell, 185–90. London: Palgrave Macmillan UK.

Lewis, J. A. 2006. "Cybersecurity and Critical Infrastructure Protection." Center for Strategic and International Studies, Washington, DC.

Lightcast Press Office. 2023. "New CyberseekTM Data Show US Is Short Nearly 530,000 Cybersecurity Workers." Lightcast Press Office, Cambridge, MA (accessed January 11, 2024), https://lightcast.io/resources/blog/cyberseek-press-release-01-24-2023.

Liu, T., E. Vergara-Cobos, and Y. Zhou. 2019. "Pricing Schemes and Seller Fraud: Evidence from New York City Taxi Rides." *Journal of Industrial Economics* 67 (1): 56–90.

Matheu, S. N., J. L. Hernandez-Ramos, A. F. Skarmeta, and G. Baldini. 2020. "A Survey of Cybersecurity Certification for the Internet of Things." *ACM Computing Surveys* 53 (6): 1–36.

Microsoft. 2021. "Microsoft Digital Defense Report 2021." Microsoft, Redmond, WA. https://query.prod.cms.rt.microsoft.com/cms/api/am/binary/RWMFIi.

Misheva, G. 2023. "Mind the Cyber Skills Gap: A Deep-Dive." Digital Skills & Jobs Platform, European Union. https://digital-skills-jobs.europa.eu/en/latest/briefs/mind-cyber-skills -gap-deep-dive.

Moore, T. 2010. "Introducing the Economics of Cybersecurity: Principles and Policy Options." In *Proceedings of a Workshop on Deterring Cyberattacks: Informing Strategies and Developing Options for US Policy*, 3–23. Washington, DC: National Academies Press.

Moore, T., and R. Anderson. 2011. "Economics and Internet Security: A Survey of Recent Analytical, Empirical, and Behavioral Research." Harvard Computer Science Group Technical Report TR-03-11, Harvard University, Cambridge, MA.

Moteff, J. D., C. Copeland, J. W. Fischer, and Resources, Science, and Industry Division. 2003. "Critical Infrastructures: What Makes an Infrastructure Critical?" Congressional Research Service, Library of Congress, Washington, DC.

Ponemon Institute. 2022. "The 2022 Data Risk in the Third-Party Ecosystem Study." Ponemon Institute, Traverse City, MI.

Rains, T. 2023. *Cybersecurity Threats, Malware Trends, and Strategies: Discover Risk Mitigation Strategies for Modern Threats to Your Organization*. Birmingham, UK: Packt Publishing Ltd.

Sarker, I. H. 2023. "Multi-Aspects AI-Based Modeling and Adversarial Learning for Cybersecurity Intelligence and Robustness: A Comprehensive Overview." *Security and Privacy* 6 (5): e295.

SecurityScorecard and Cyentia. 2024. "Close Encounters of the Third (and Fourth) Party Kind." SecurityScorecard, New York.

Shafqat, N., and A. Masood. 2016. "Comparative Analysis of Various National Cyber Security Strategies." *International Journal of Computer Science and Information Security* 14 (1): 129–36.

Sultan, A. 2019. "Improving Cybersecurity Awareness in Underserved Populations." Center for Long-Term Cybersecurity, University of California, Berkeley. https://cltc.berkeley.edu /wpcontent/uploads/2019/04/CLTC_Underserved_Populations.

Thakur, M. 2024. "Cyber Security Threats and Countermeasures in Digital Age." *Journal of Applied Science and Education* 4 (1): 1–20.

Verified Market Reports. 2023. "Government Cyber Security Market Size 2021 to 2023." Verified Market Research, Washington, DC. https://www.verifiedmarketreports.com /product/government-cyber-security-market/.

Weber, V., M. Pericàs Riera, and E. Laumann. 2023. "Mapping the World's Critical Infrastructure Sectors." DGAP Policy Brief No. 35, German Council on Foreign Relations, Berlin.

WEF (World Economic Forum). 2024. *Global Cybersecurity Outlook 2024*. Geneva: WEF. https://www.weforum.org/reports/global-cybersecurity-outlook-2024.

Westlands Advisory. 2023. "Industrial Cybersecurity Industry Analysis." Westlands Advisory, Richmond, UK.

The White House. 2023a. "Federal Cybersecurity Research and Development Strategic Plan." The White House, Washington, DC. https://www.whitehouse.gov/wp-content/uploads /2024/01/Federal-Cybersecurity-RD-Strategic-Plan-2023.pdf and https://www.whitehouse .gov/wp-content/uploads/2022/03/ap_16_it_fy2023.pdf.

The White House. 2023b. "US National Cybersecurity Strategy." The White House, Washington, DC.

World Bank. 2023. "Strengthening Cybersecurity and Resilience of Critical Infrastructure: Insights from the Republic of Korea and Other Digital Nations." World Bank Korea Office Innovation and Technology Note, World Bank, Washington, DC.

Zwilling, M., G. Klien, D. Lesjak, Ł. Wiechetek, F. Cetin, and H. N. Basim. 2022. "Cyber Security Awareness, Knowledge and Behavior: A Comparative Study." *Journal of Computer Information Systems* 62 (1): 82–97.

Conclusion

As major cyber incidents become more frequent, the ability to safeguard the operability of systems is challenged by a limited understanding of their nature. The seemingly irregular patterns followed by cyber incidents foster a perception that such events are inevitable and unnecessary to study in depth. This book challenges this view by embracing the inherent complexity, uncertainty, and nonlinearity of chaotic systems, and identifying the characteristics, trends, determinants, and socioeconomic effects of disclosed cyber incidents worldwide. Thus, the book offers pioneering insights from the cybersecurity landscape and adaptive strategies, flexible policies, and decentralized governance efforts to foster innovation and sustainability amid ongoing change and uncertainty.

Yet, more research is needed for further understanding the underlying principles of cyberspace as an evolving system. These efforts can lead to better prediction and management strategies, helping to anticipate significant changes or incidents; the design of more robust and resilient digital infrastructure and security systems; improved efficiency of proactive cybersecurity measures; and better and more informed policy making. However, to move forward on a research agenda, stakeholders must first address the issue of the scarcity of comprehensive and reliable data on cyber incidents and their subsequent economic and social ramifications. Data play a crucial role in the study of cybersecurity as they are essential for modeling and simulation, understanding the threat dynamics, testing hypotheses around cybersecurity measures, detecting trends, improving predictability, and controlling outcomes, especially large negative impacts to socioeconomic progress. Addressing data scarcity involves confronting policies related to the reporting of cyber incidents and understanding their impact on the economic performance of victims. Thus, careful policy designs are needed to encourage transparency and compliance, while also protecting the affected entities from further economic repercussions.

Moreover, it is essential to recognize cybersecurity as not merely a technical issue, but as an economic matter, crucial for human development in the digital age. This recognition underscores the need for greater involvement of economists in studying cybersecurity. Several key questions remain open for exploration in this domain. For instance, researchers could investigate how cyber incidents affect consumer behavior, development outcomes, investment decisions, and adoption of digital technologies, especially in emerging markets and developing countries. Researchers could also try to develop new ways to derive value from cybersecurity investments that overcome the complexity of modeling a cost-saving approach. Efforts could focus on understanding the issue of third-party cyber risk and the increasing dependence of societies on the correct functioning of a few private systems. In this sense, there is also a pressing need to examine the vulnerability of critical infrastructure, especially the "single points of failure" that could have cascading effects on national security, economic stability, and even the protection of human rights.

Additional topics worth exploring include the political ramifications of cyber incidents, particularly in the context of electoral processes; the effectiveness of cybersecurity awareness campaigns; the enablement effects of cybersecurity measures on the provision of public goods; and the theoretical link between physical, biological, and economic complex systems and cybersecurity economics.

Overall, advancing the understanding of these and other pertinent questions within the economics of cybersecurity is vital for developing effective policy interventions and strategies to mitigate cyber threats and promote economic resilience worldwide, and especially in developing nations.

Glossary

Critical infrastructure Systems and assets, whether physical or virtual, that are vital to the nation, and whose incapacity or destruction would have a debilitating impact on security, national economic security, national public health or safety, or any combination of those matters (NIST, n.d.).

Cyber Refers to both information and communications networks (NIST, n.d.). The prefix "cyber" is etymologically rooted in the Greek definition of *kubernetes*, which implies the interface and interaction of the biological and the mechanical (Van Puyvelde and Brantly 2019).

Cyber capability A system's potential to maintain the confidentiality, integrity, and availability of computers, networks, and their resident data or data in transit. Cyber capability is a combination of mutually reinforced technical, physical, and procedural controllers and measures (NIST, n.d.; Van Puyvelde and Brantly 2019).

Cyber incident or cyber event An event or the end result of any single unauthorized effort taken using an information system (for example, computer technology) or network that resulted in an actual or potentially nationally relevant adverse effect on any of the three layers that constitute cyberspace, including information systems, networks, and/or the information residing therein (Harry and Gallagher 2023; NIST, n.d.).

Cyber incident response Response to threats and the mitigation of violations of cybersecurity policies and recommended practices. Incident response allows victims to detect, contain, and recover from security incidents (NIST, n.d.; Taddeo 2019; Woods et al. 2023).

Cyber risk "Risk" describes possible negative consequences (harm) weighted by the probability of occurrence, and "cyber" restricts the scope to incidents caused by logical (as opposed to physical) force (Woods and Böhme 2021). The harm could be related to the loss of confidentiality, integrity, or availability of information, data, or information (or control) systems and reflect the potential adverse impacts on organizational operations (mission, functions, image, or reputation) and assets, individuals, other organizations, and the nation (NIST, n.d.).

Cyber threat Any circumstance or event with the potential to have an adverse impact on victims' operations in cyberspace. It is also the potential for a threat source to exploit a particular information system vulnerability successfully (NIST, n.d.).

Cyberattack Malicious activity attempting (successfully or not) to gain control of an information system without permission, to disrupt, collect, disable, destroy, degrade, or deny information system infrastructure or the information itself (NIST, n.d.).

Cyberattack surface The set of points on the boundary of a cyber system, a cyber system element, or a cyber environment where an attacker can try to enter, cause an effect on, or extract data from that system, system element, or environment (NIST, n.d.).

Cybersecurity Systemic security in cyberspace to ensure the availability, integrity, authentication, confidentiality, and nonrepudiation of all components of cyberspace, including systems, information, and data. Instruments for achieving cybersecurity include any technology, measure, or practice that aims at preventing cyber incidents or mitigating their impact (IBM 2023; Van Puyvelde and Brantly 2019).

Cybersecurity awareness A learning process that aims to focus attention on security and change individual and organizational attitudes to realize the importance of cybersecurity and the adverse consequences of its failure (NIST, n.d.).

Cybersecurity domains At a high level of abstraction, cybersecurity goods and services can be bundled into robustness of digital systems (secured by design systems), resilience of digital systems (sustainable systems), and incident response capabilities (Taddeo 2019).

Cybersecurity resilience The ability of an information system to continue to: (1) operate under adverse conditions or stress, even if in a degraded or debilitated state, while maintaining essential operational capabilities; and (2) recover to an effective operational posture in a timeframe consistent with mission needs (NIST, n.d.).

Cybersecurity robustness The ability of cybersecurity measures to operate correctly and reliably across a wide range of operational conditions, including threats (NIST, n.d.). Robustness is also described as the difference between the expected and actual behavior of a system (Taddeo 2019).

Cyberspace A physical and virtual domain on a par with the other domains of land, sea, air, and space, which allows for human interactions and forms the foundation of modern life. Unlike its counterpart domains, cyberspace is entirely made by humans whose interactions form a giant grid of networks called "cyberspace," which depends on physical, logical (code), and human structures to operate. The centrality of humans in cyberspace makes social scientific approaches essential to its study. This comprehensive definition was formed by blending descriptions from academic scholars and government agencies, like the US Department of Defense, Van Puyvelde and Brantly (2019), and Demchak and Dombrowski (2013).

Cyberspace layers The cyber persona (user), logical (code), and physical (infrastructure) layers.

Disruptive cyber incident A cyber incident that impedes the normal operation of the targeted information systems (Harry and Gallagher 2018).

Exploitive cyber incident A cyber incident designed to access or exfiltrate information from information systems illicitly (Harry and Gallagher 2018).

Threat intelligence Threat information that has been aggregated, transformed, analyzed, interpreted, or enriched to provide the necessary context for decision-making processes (NIST, n.d.).

Vulnerability Weakness in an information system, application, network, system security procedures, internal controls, or implementation that could be exploited or triggered by a threat source (NIST, n.d.).

References

Demchak, C., and P. Dombrowski. 2013. "Cyber Westphalia: Asserting State Prerogatives in Cyberspace." *Georgetown Journal of International Affairs* (2013–14): 29–38.

Harry, C., and N. Gallagher. 2018. "Classifying Cyber Events." *Journal of Information Warfare* 17 (3): 17–31.

Harry, C., and N. W. Gallagher. 2023. "Categorizing Cyber Effects." In *The Elgar Companion to Digital Transformation, Artificial Intelligence and Innovation in the Economy, Society and Democracy*, edited by E. G. Carayannis, E. Grigoroudis, D. F. J. Campbell, and S. K. Katsikas, 7–31. Edward Elgar Publishing.

IBM. 2023. "What Is Cybersecurity?" IBM, Armonk, NY. https://www.ibm.com/topics /cybersecurity.

NIST (National Institute of Standards and Technology). n.d. "NIST Glossary." NIST, Gaithersburg, MD. https://csrc.nist.gov/glossary/.

Taddeo, M. 2019. "Is Cybersecurity a Public Good?" *Minds and Machines* 29: 349–54.

Van Puyvelde, D., and A. F. Brantly. 2019. *Cybersecurity: Politics, Governance and Conflict in Cyberspace*. John Wiley & Sons.

Woods, D. W., and R. Böhme. 2021. "SoK: Quantifying Cyber Risk." In *2021 IEEE Symposium on Security and Privacy (SP)*, 211–28. Piscataway, NJ: Institute of Electrical and Electronics Engineers.

Woods, D. W., R. Böhme, J. Wolff, and D. Schwarcz. 2023. "Lessons Lost: Incident Response in the Age of Cyber Insurance and Breach Attorneys." In *32nd USENIX Security Symposium (USENIX Security 23)*, 2259–73. Berkeley, CA: USENIX.